RELIGION AND ART
SHAPING THE WORLD FOR CHRIST

Religion and Art
Shaping the World for Christ

Copyright 2023 Mark David Harris

All Rights Reserved

No part of this book may be reproduced or stored in a retrieval system, or transmitted in any form or by any means, electronic, mechanical, photocopying, recording, or otherwise, without the express written permission of the publisher.

Cover design by Nancy Harris
Image used under license from Shutterstock.com

MD Harris Institute Publishing

Daniels, WV

eBook ISBN 978-1-7343617-6-6

Print ISBN 978-1-7343617-7-3

TABLE OF CONTENTS

Introduction 1
1. What does it mean to shape the world? 4
2. What is art, and what are its characteristics, including religious and Christian Art? 23
3. Overview of Major Religions and Philosophies 37
4. How do Muslims use the arts to shape the world? 52
5. How do Hindus use the arts to shape the world? 62
6. How do Buddhists use the arts to shape the world? 70
7. How do other religionists and secular groups use the arts to shape the world? 80
8. What is the Biblical basis for using the Arts in Christian ministry? 90
9. How can Christians use the Arts as others have to shape the world for Christ? 99
10. Using the arts to shape the world for Christ in the Roman Empire (30-400s) 104
11. Using the arts to shape the world for Christ in the Middle Ages (500s-1300s) 110
12. Using the Arts to shape the world for Christ in the Renaissance and Reformation (1300s-1600s) 118
13. Using the arts to shape the world for Christ in the Modern Era (1700s to today) 124
14. How do the arts help shape the world for Christ? By teaching ethics and morality 129

15 How do the arts help shape the world for Christ? By building communities 136

16 How do the Arts help shape the world for Christ? by revealing the person of God 142

17 How do the Arts help shape the world for Christ? By meeting human needs 152

18 Conclusion 158

Appendix 1 Summaries of Religions and Philosophies 160

Appendix 2 Great Works of Christian Art 170

Appendix 3 Using this book in sermons, classrooms, and other teaching occasions. 175

Bibliography 177

INTRODUCTION

The minutes, hours, days, and years of life stay the same from millennia to millennia, but the number of activities continues to grow. Science and mathematics have enabled mankind to measure almost everything, and since we can, we do. Inevitably, we judge ourselves on the quantity and (measurable) quality of what we do each day. If we feel we are winning, we let others know, subtly or unsubtly. If we feel we are losing, we hide.

On this existential treadmill, or as Hindus might say the Samsara, the cycle of birth, death, and rebirth, we strive to be productive in every area of life. We have little time and less patience for things and people that reduce our perceived productivity, like animals, children, and the aged, who can't or don't have the same direction or move as fast as we do.

Most people pretend to maintain the pace, and the image we want to portray, in the modern world. In reality, none can maintain the pace or the pretense for long. Some call this the Rat Race. The Eagles song *Life in the Fast Lane* captures the fast-moving prison in which most of us serve a life sentence.[1]

> Eager for action, hot for the game
> The coming attraction, the drop of a name
> They knew all the right people, they took all the right pills

---

[1] Joe Walsh, Glenn Frey, and Don Henley, *Life in the Fast Lane* (Eagles, 1976), https://www.lyrics.com/track/22158035/Eagles/Life+in+the+Fast+Lane.

Religion and Art

> They threw outrageous parties, they paid heavenly bills
> There were lines on the mirror, lines on her face
> She pretended not to notice, she was caught up in the race
> Out every evening, until it was light
> He was too tired to make it, she was too tired to fight about it
> Life in the fast lane, surely make you lose your mind
> Life in the fast lane, huh
> Life in the fast lane, everything all the time
> Life in the fast lane, uh-huh

Growing weary of the race, people wander, looking for meaning beyond bank balances, corner offices, impressive titles, and to-do lists. The world looks for answers, and philosophy, political activism, and religion promise to provide them. One of the chief ways that philosophy, politics, and religion do so is through the arts.

The arts include music, drama, dance, visual arts (painting, sculpture, etc.), and others. The arts appeal to the mind and to the emotions. The arts touch all five senses and overwhelm us with grandeur, or revulsion. The arts shape how we think and feel in ways visible and invisible, logical and illogical, conscious and unconscious, good and evil.

The Church also competes for the hearts and minds of the people of the world in the marketplace of ideas. As people of the Bible, we use Holy Scripture as Paul commands in 2 Timothy 3:16-17, which reads, "All scripture is given by inspiration of God, and is profitable for doctrine, for reproof, for correction, for instruction in righteousness: That the man of God may be perfect, thoroughly furnished unto all good works."[2] The word of God, the Bible, is the sword of the Spirit, mightier than any force on earth to bring people to know and love God. The Church will succeed in

---

[2] All scripture is KJV unless otherwise noted.

Introduction

every task for which the Lord has commissioned it, no matter what pollsters, politicians, pundits, prognosticators, and pagans predict.

In our work of winning disciples for Christ, however, we neglect a potent influencer, the arts. The arts touch the soul as reason enlivens the mind. Justifiably afraid of idolatry, we deny ourselves a powerful weapon in the arsenal of truth.

This book examines art in many forms. It then provides an overview of religion and philosophy, and considers how philosophers, political activists, and religious adherents have used art to portray and shape the world to their liking. Next, this book looks at the experience of the Church with the arts. It encourages churches and Christians to recover the arts in their sanctified fullness and use them to shape the world for Christ. The arts offer a path to meaning and wholeness in ways that reason cannot. Reclaiming the arts will help the Church reclaim a portion of its power to glorify God in the world. That is what this book is all about.

1

WHAT DOES IT MEAN TO SHAPE THE WORLD?

Several of the girls in our youth choir gasped when they entered the Notre Dame Cathedral in Montreal. The colors, the lights and the architecture were breathtaking, and several of our chattiest young ladies stood in amazed silence. Boys, too, slowed down at the spectacle. Coming from a Baptist church, most of these kids had never seen such beauty in religious art. One girl told me that if she went to this church, she would never be able to listen to the sermon. Others said that the cathedral made them feel the overwhelming presence of God. Time seemed to stop.

Serving in the Army and living throughout the United States and Europe, I have walked the Stations of the Cross at the Kreuzberg monastery, marveled at the ceiling of the Sistine Chapel, and enjoyed the peace and beauty of the garden and cloister at Mont Saint Michel. I have toured the Benedictine Abbey of Frauenworth, explored the Church of the Holy Sepulcher in Jerusalem, and studied masterpieces at the Louvre. Our youth were right; beauty can be distracting, but it can also be profoundly worshipful. Coming from a Protestant tradition, I am accustomed to churches with little notable architecture and even less art. We are missing something. Beyond doubt, the arts can glorify God.

My wife plays flute, my oldest daughter piano and violin, my oldest son French Horn, piano, and accordion, my middle daughter flute, and my youngest daughter trombone and piano. My youngest son sings, and I dabble in guitar, piano, trumpet, and voice. Together we have spent many hours as a family enjoying ourselves and honoring God through the music we create and share.

The Arts in the Pre-Modern World

In parts of the Protestant world, many of the arts have been neglected or despised for centuries. Puritan churches considered even the cross to be an idol, and many early Baptist churches did not have one. Early Baptists preferred "meeting houses," with Palladian (Georgian) architecture, for their assembly areas. The first Baptist church in America, established by Roger Williams (1603-1683) in Providence, Rhode Island in 1638, is a good example. J. Stanley Lemons writes of the updated church, built in 1775,

> The building is dignified in its restrained ornamentation, but the classical details were standard pattern book designs, common to Georgian style buildings of the 18th century. While the building retained some of its form from Anglican churches, it retained at least three major elements of the New England meeting house style. First, it was square, 80x80 feet. Second, it lacked iconography: no stained glass, no statues, not even a cross. The Baptists were quite conscientious in their exclusion of religious symbols, including the cross itself. The Puritans were thorough iconoclasts, and the Baptists of Rhode Island maintained that tradition even as they constructed an elegant building. Third, the high pulpit was placed against the wall and

centered in order to emphasize the preaching of the Word and to banish the idea of an altar.[3]

The example of the First Baptist Church in America was reproduced thousands of times in early American Protestantism. Images, theater, and many other arts were excluded. Only in music, with works by geniuses like Bach and Handel, did Protestant churches achieve artistic grandeur. Musicians have historically been encouraged to use their gifts in church for the glory of God, while other artists have been told to practice their craft elsewhere.

Even music, though, has been controversial in the Church. The early Church adopted much from the Jewish musical tradition, singing the Psalms and the Canticles during worship. Instrumental music and dance, however, were generally shunned by early believers due to their association with pagan worship.[4] The Catholic Church discouraged certain types of polyphony on the grounds that it could obscure the words or confuse people about the unity of God.[5] Pope John XXII issued the Decretal Letter Extravagans Communis in 1324 to clarify the official position, which was directed towards the clergy, not the laity.[6] Some prominent musicians of the Church rejected the augmented fourth (diminished fifth) interval (F to B, C to F#, A to Eb, etc.), also known as a tritone or *Diabolus in Musica*, for not reflecting the beauty of God. In the modern day, composers from Bernstein (*West Side Story*) to Wagner (*Tristan and Isolde*) have used this

---

[3] J Stanley Lemons, *First: The First Baptist Church in America* (Providence, RI: Charitable Baptist Society, 2001), 26.
[4] Andrew Wilson-Dickson, *The Story of Christian Music*, (Oxford, England: Lion Publishing, 1992), 28.
[5] Daniel J. Levitin, *This is your Brain on Music, the Science of a Human Obsession*, (New York: Penguin Group, 2006), 12.
[6] EXTRAVAGANS COMMUNIS, Concerning the life and the decency of the Clergy, https://cappellagregoriana.files.wordpress.com/2017/06/docta-sanctorum-en1.pdf.

extremely dissonant sound to communicate tension, longing, and defiance.[7]

The earliest mention of musical instruments in the Bible occurs when Jubal is described as "the father of all who played stringed instruments and pipes" (Genesis 4:21). David played instruments, and "spoke to the chiefs of the Levites to appoint their relatives, the singers, with instruments of music, harps, lyres, loud-sounding cymbals, to raise sounds of joy" (1 Chronicles 15:16). Temple musicians used cymbals, harps, and lyres (1 Chronicles 25). Music was an indispensable part of Jewish worship. Worshippers are specifically told to praise the Lord with musical instruments (Psalm 150). Jewish exiles in Babylon were ridiculed by their Babylonian masters, who forced them to "Sing us one of the songs of Zion" even though the Babylonian army had destroyed Zion (Psalm 137:3).

Visual arts also had a place in Hebrew life. Dated around 1400 BC, Exodus 25 to 31 describes in detail how the former slaves were commanded to build the Tabernacle, the tent which would house the presence of God during their wanderings in the Sinai desert and into the Promised Land. God's instructions for the building of His Temple, around 970 BC, were equally specific, and the results equally ornate (1 Kings 6, 1 Chronicles 28-29). Four centuries later, the Babylonian King Nebuchadnezzar conquered Judea and destroyed Jerusalem and the Temple. Hoping to prevent the restive Jews from rising again, Nebuchadnezzar deported all the leaders, merchants, and leading men of Israel. The artists and craftsmen, cultural innovators that could incite the Hebrews to rebellion, also walked to Babylon at the point of a spear (2 Kings 24:10-16).

---

[7] Judith Kogan, The Unsettling Sound Of Tritones, The Devil's Interval, https://www.npr.org/2017/10/31/560843189/the-unsettling-sound-of-tritones-the-devils-interval.

The use of the arts, and controversy over the role of the arts, in the Church continued through the Middle Ages and into the Reformation. For Martin Luther (1483-1546), music was "instilled into the fabric of the world," organically related to mathematics as a key component of creation.[8] As such, he promoted music in the churches. Luther wrote Christian words for German folk tunes, composed music himself (*Ein Feste Burg Ist Unser Gott*),[9] wrote lyrics (possibly *Away in a Manger*), and allowed instruments to accompany singing.[10] By contrast, John Calvin (1509-1564) did not speak of the grand metaphysical tradition of music.[11] He saw music as an aide to rhetoric. Calvin felt that congregational singing was important, and he supervised the compilation of the Genevan Psalter, which includes 126 melodies designed to be sung with metrical translations of the 150 psalms. However, he only allowed the unison singing of Psalms in his Geneva churches. Harmony, polyphony, and instruments were forbidden.[12]

The Arts in the Modern World

The Industrial Revolution of the 19th century changed how man produced the goods he needed to live and to thrive. Productivity was measured by how many shirts or wheels or nails could be produced in a period of time (typically an hour or a day). Prices fell, making more things available to the masses and raising standards of living all over Europe, America, and eventually the

---

[8] Jeremy Begbie, *Music, Modernity, and God: Essays in Listening* (Oxford: Oxford University Press, 2013), 31.
[9] A Mighty Fortress is Our God.
[10] Wilson-Dickson, 62-63.
[11] The metaphysical tradition of music suggests that musical sound, especially harmony, is related to and describes the cosmic order. This tradition springs from the Pythagorean notions of musical intervals as related to mathematical ratios and enters Christianity in the writings of Augustine. It was widely accepted in the Middle Ages, but lost currency in and after the Enlightenment.
[12] Begbie, 19.

rest of the world. But industrialization also changed how man thought about the goods he was producing, and the effective use of his time. Quality retained its importance, but individuality and beauty did not. Goods and later even services became commodities. Machine-produced clothing and furniture that were cheap but "good enough" replaced handmade clothing and unique furniture designed and produced by expert artisans but costing far more. As my mother was growing up in Arkansas in the 1940s, a "store bought" shirt was a special treat, and homemade clothes were often considered drab and ordinary.

Production by machine for the masses rather than production by people for a select group also impacted the arts. When Jane Austin wrote *Pride and Prejudice*, music was created in the home by one or more family members singing and often playing one or more instruments. Wealthy households like the Bennets might have had a piano forte. Poor households, like the Pontipees in *Seven Brides for Seven Brothers*, might have had a guitar, or a saw and a jug. But everyone had a voice and most people made music. Music could also be created in the local church, as was the case when Hans Gruber and Josef Mohr wrote the Christmas carol, *Silent Night*.

Technology advanced, and vinyl albums, tapes, compact discs (CD), and digital files brought the best and/or the most popular music in the world to anyone with the technological capability to listen. As record players, tape decks, CD players, and smart phones spread through the global population, professional and globally produced music replaced amateur and locally produced music. This situation is suggested by the fact that in 1900, 364,545 new pianos were sold in the United States.[13] In 2007, 62,536 new pianos were sold. This drop occurred despite the

---

[13] Blue Book of Pianos, "US Piano Sales History from 1900 to Present," www.bluebookofpianos.com, 2012, http://www.bluebookofpianos.com/uspiano.htm.

fact that the total US population in 1900 was 76 million, while in 2007 it was 303 million. For a variety of reasons, street music nearly vanished. Musicians of all sorts, peripatetic poetic street vendors and the musical cries of city watchmen produced a melodic cacophony of sounds in Elizabethan London.[14] Car horns, engine noise, sirens, occasional voices produce a cacophony in modern New York City. Car radios, computers, televisions, and smartphones with ear buds, both private and public, deliver much of the music one hears.

The Arts in the Modern Church

Against this cultural backdrop, many feel that the Western World is losing its Christian tradition. Westerners don't know the Gospel and may have never heard the name of Jesus Christ. Legions of self-described Christians are biblically illiterate.[15] Humans across the globe search for guidance and meaning from secularism and related philosophies, one of the world religions, political action as religion, or from a host of splinter groups. Local churches often feel powerless. Sometimes Christians fear that every other group, from Animist to Zoroastrian, is reaching more people than the people of Jesus are.

Discouraged Christians hold that the Church in Europe and the United States is retreating.[16] While Western believers thrill to

---

[14] Bruce Johnson, "From Music to Noise: The Decline of Street Music." *Nineteenth-Century Music Review* 15, no. 1 (February 6, 2017): 67–78. https://doi.org/10.1017/s147940981700009x.
[15] Kenneth Berding, "The Crisis of Biblical Illiteracy." *Biola Magazine*, June 2014.
   http://magazine.biola.edu/article/14-spring/the-crisis-of-biblical-illiteracy/.
[16] Seems to be, but actually is not. God will not allow His Church to fail. Secularists desperately hope that religion will fade away with the advance of technology and material prosperity, but it will not. Those leaving the church today are by and large those nominal "Christians" who were never really believers at all.

stories of revivals in Africa, Asia, and Latin America, we despair at falling attendance, empty sanctuaries, and hostility in our own societies. Years ago, a military chaplain told me that since he could not compete with movies, music, smart phones, and the internet, it was hard to even try.

As early as the 1940s, Reverend H. Boone Porter (1923-1999) lamented that the Western church was relinquishing its cultural leadership to the secularists. Feeling that mental images, not theological formulae, make up human spiritual experience, he advocated using fine arts to "stimulate, harmonize, and integrate the imagination."[17] Lloyd Arnett, a professor at Trinity Western University, writes that theater is a God-given gift, recognizable in all cultures and of benefit to all mankind. It is the place for ideas, philosophies, and discussions of man's fate.[18]

Since before the days of Moses, believers in Jehovah have used the arts, like painting, sculpture, drama, dance, food, textiles, and music, to communicate truth and shape the world around them. The arts can help modern day Christians and churches address the problems we face. They can lead people to Jesus, build up believers, and influence the thinking and actions of the larger world. This book does the following:

1. Discusses the characteristics of art, including religious and Christian Art
2. Notes how Muslims, Hindus, Buddhists, other religionists, and secular groups including humanists, Marxists, and postmodern Critical Theorists, use the arts to shape the world.
3. Establishes the biblical basis for using the arts in ministry.

---

[17] Harry Boone. Porter, "God, Art, and Satan," *Anglican Theological Review*, 29, no. 4 (October 1947): 242-246.
[18] Lloyd Arnett, "The Sacred Precinct: Reclaiming the Place of the Christian Humanist Tradition of Theatre Art in the 21st Century Intellectual Community," *Baylor Journal of Theatre and Performance* 1, no. 1 (Fall 2004): 69-76, http://www.jstor.org/stable/44804945.

4. Shows how Christians in the Roman Empire (30 to 400s), Middle Ages (500s to 1300s), Renaissance and Reformation (1300s to 1600s), and the Modern Period (1700s to today), used the arts to shape the world for Christ.
5. Demonstrates how the arts can teach ethics and morality, help build communities, help reveal the person of God and help meet human needs.

Most participants in a discussion tacitly assume that everyone involved agrees with the definitions of the terms that they use. Doing so is a recipe for confusion, misunderstanding, and strife. Before proceeding, we must describe, if not define, our terms. In the interest of time, space, and peace, the following are working descriptions and are not intended to be authoritative in all contexts.

The Church refers to the body of all Christians, past, present, and future. It includes Catholics, Protestants, Orthodox, and others. The local church describes a group of believers that meet in a specific place and at a certain time and worship together. The local church interacts directly with people and families, the fundamental unit of every society, who are themselves local. Aside from the family, the local church is the preeminent organization to accomplish God's work in the world. Not only all politics, but all life, is local. Parachurch organizations generally do not have congregations like churches but exist to support the Church, local churches, and individual Christians in their lives and ministries. Many Christian groups have regional, national, and even global church hierarchies. These provide resources, guidance, consultation, and oversight, but nevertheless lack the impact of the local church in the lives of its members.

Shaping the World

The phrase "shaping the world" demands some explanation. Everyone tries to modify their world for their own benefit. We build or buy houses and furnish them to maximize our convenience and pleasure. We find jobs that we enjoy, or at least tolerate, and that will pay us enough money to survive, and hopefully thrive. We find friends and marriage partners that give us the most satisfaction. We wear clothing, decorate our environment, and post items on social media in ways that we believe will make us feel good about ourselves and look good to others. Restated, we shape the world around us for our benefit.

Businesses employ workers, produce goods and services, advertise, and portray themselves favorably in every possible way. Religious groups attempt to display their piety and power. Governments spend most of their time trying to look good. Organizations do the same.

Animals are no exception, finding burrows and building nests for their survival and pleasure. Peacocks display their plumage to seduce peahens of their choice, and bucks compete with other bucks to mate with the most desirable does. Ultimately, every sentient creature tries to shape the world for its personal benefit.

Art varies in how it shapes the world. Modern art, such as Monet's *Water Lilies* disorients us, while Tracey Emin's *My Bed* invokes nausea and pity. Emin mirrors much of the art in the late modern era, shaping the world in favor of confusion, meaninglessness, weakness, and despair. Much politically themed art, such as suffragette and feminist art, does the same. The Preacher in Ecclesiastes, describing life without God, could relate.

Art can encourage morality or immorality. The 1949 film *Mother is a Freshman* depicts a widow returning to college, falling in love, and confirming the value of the traditional family and education. Like Bob Hope and Bing Crosby movies of the time, it remains upbeat and clean.[19] The Motion Picture Production Code (1934-1954) ensured that Hollywood films of the day encouraged people to be decent, polite, and fashionable.[20] Movies depicted and inspired the best, not the worst, in humanity.

Arts can encourage or discourage personal discipline. The effort involved in learning an instrument or writing a story not only produces skills but also instills habits of self-discipline which will lead to future accomplishments. Beginning artists copy the work of masters, placing themselves under the authority of and modeling exemplary artists rather than ordinary or even poor ones. Jazz musician Charlie Parker was renowned for improvisation, but he could only perform his brilliant work once he had mastered his saxophone. Likewise, artistic creativity fully blossoms when discipline has dug the roots and grown the trunk of the tree.

Discipline is required to appreciate art as much as it is to produce art.[21] Listening to a three-minute popular song on guitar and piano does not train an ear and a mind like listening to a twenty-minute classical score performed by a symphony orchestra. Ballet is beautiful to the beholder but punishing to the performer. Visitors to the Louvre who have artistic knowledge and discipline study the Mona Lisa, lingering for minutes to drink in every detail. Those without the requisite knowledge and discipline glance, check it off their list, and keep walking.

---

[19] Tiffany Brannan, "Popcorn and Inspiration: 'Mother Is a Freshman' (1949): Lighthearted Film Endorses Higher Education," *The Epoch Times*, July 21, 2020.
[20] Motion Picture Production Code, https://www.jstor.org/stable/1026152.
[21] Carol Reynolds, "Virtue and Discipline in the Arts," *Memoria Press*, July 26, 2021, https://www.memoriapress.com/articles/virtue-discipline-arts/.

Non-Christian views shaping the World

The human heart abhors a vacuum. If Christians do not teach and live the worldview exemplified by Christ, others will teach and live non-Christian and anti-Christian worldviews.[22] People in varying cultures throughout time have held vastly different opinions on key beliefs. Science, logic, and the arts can promote non-Christian worldviews to others who have not yet decided what to believe.[23]

For example, many secularists assume that the equality of all people, individual liberty, and free speech are "self-evident." While equality, liberty, and freedom of expression were self-evident to the signers of the American Declaration of Independence, these concepts are not found in many societies. Ancient civilizations from Aztec to Zulu did not hold that all men are created equal.

Islam divides the world into the *umma*, the Muslim community, the *dhimmi*, non-Muslims living under Muslim political control, and the *kafir* (infidels), everyone else on earth.[24] Classical Muslims expected and taught that Islam would gain

---

[22] Followers of Christ are not afraid of non-Christian or anti-Christian world views for our own sake. Christianity is true and God is sovereign. His Church will ultimately prevail against all enemies. The gates of hell will not stand against His people in His power. Eventually, every knee shall bow, and every tongue confess, that Jesus Christ is Lord. Rather, Christians have been saved by totally unmerited grace, and in gratitude for our salvation, we want to share God's love with others.

[23] Mongol emperor Kublai Khan asked the Catholic Church to send 100 missionaries to his court to educate him about Christianity in AD 1269. Pope Clement IV had died in 1268 and the election of Gregory X didn't happen until 1271. Due to the interval, and the fact that it was hard to find missionaries, the Church did not send help. Kublai Khan became Buddhist. After the division of the Mongol empire, most Mongols became Muslim.
https://worldhistoryconnected.press.uillinois.edu/12.2/forum_may.html#_edn6.

[24] Seyyed Hossein Nasr, *The Study Quran: A New Translation and Commentary* (New York: HarperOne, 2017), Quran 4:92, notes pp 234-235. Quran 9:29, and many others.

political control of every nation on earth. At that time, all the *kafir* would eventually either join the *umma* or be members of the *dhimmi* by default. Many contemporary Muslims hold this expectation as well.

When Islam speaks of the equality of mankind, it is referring to the equality of everyone in the *umma*, not of every human on earth. Islam, as revealed in the *Sahih al Muslim, the Book of Destiny*, teaches that all babies are born Muslim, and thereby are born equal, but many reject Islam and therefore lose their equal status.[25] The "peace" promised in Islam is only the peace for Muslims. *Dhimmi* are oppressed and *kafirs*, considered members of the *Dar al Harb* (House of War) are attacked (sooner or later).[26] Certainly, some Muslims believe that all people are equal, but this belief is not consistent with a traditional interpretation of Islam's guiding documents.[27]

The Hindu caste system divides humanity into five groups: the *Brahmins* (religious leaders), the *Kshatriya* (political and military leaders), the *Vaishyas* (merchants and farmers), the *Shudras* (menial laborers), and the *Dalits* (untouchables, those outside the caste system).[28] Hindus are born into a position in the caste, and no matter what their accomplishments, cannot escape their caste in this life. A Hindu's only hope is to accumulate enough merit to be reborn into a higher caste, or to escape the

---

[25] The Book of Destiny, *Sahih al Muslim*, Book 46, Hadith 37, https://sunnah.com/muslim/46.
[26] Majid Khadduri, *The Islamic Conception of Justice* (Baltimore: Johns Hopkins University Press, 2003), 163-171
[27] "Traditional" in this context means authorial intent. The sources of the Quran and the Hadiths meant to communicate something in their writings. It is our responsibility as recipients of these writings to understand what their intent was in sending these to us. This book uses the authorial intent hermeneutic throughout. The reader response hermeneutic is decidedly secondary.
[28] Rig Veda, Hymn 10:90 Purusha, Ralph T H Griffith, Arthur Berriedale Keith, and Jon William Fergus, The Vedas : The Saṃhitās of the Ṛig, Yajur (White and Black), Sāma, and Atharva Vedas (United States? Kshetra Books, 2017).

samsara, the cycle of birth and death, by achieving *moksha*, release into paradise. Hinduism, as revealed in the *Vedas*, the ten principal *Upanishads*, and the *Bhagavad Gita*, attributes a person's station in their present life to their actions, good or bad, in this life and in past lives.[29] If someone is sick or impoverished, and/or if they are born into a low caste, it is their own fault. Some secularized Hindus hold that all people are equal, but that message is not consistent with the core scriptures of Hinduism.

Buddhism posits a basic equality among *Bhikkhu* (monks) but not among *Bhikkhuni* (nuns) in the *Sangha* (Buddhist monastic system).[30] The Buddha was reluctant to admit women to the Sangha and once he relented, he placed the nuns strictly under the monks.[31] After relenting, he predicted trouble for Buddhism because women were included.[32] *Bhikkhuni* have been in the *Mahayana* Buddhist tradition since the beginning, but not in the *Theraveda* Buddhist traditions for centuries until the 2010s. Only recently have nuns been ordained in the *Vajrayana* (Tibetan) tradition. Laymen and laywomen rank below their clerical compatriots in Buddhism, as they are typically more lives away from *moksha*, which is enlightenment or the release into *Nirvana*. As with Hinduism, the hard logic in Buddhism is that humans get exactly what they deserve based on their thoughts, words, and actions in previous lives. As with Islam and Hinduism, some Buddhists undoubtedly believe in the equality of man. However, a traditional interpretation of fundamental Buddhist beliefs does not support such a belief.

If so many religions and cultures do not teach the equality of all mankind, why do so many nations and people today believe

---

[29] Eknath Easwaran, *The Upanishads* (ReadHowYouWant.com, 2010), 114-115.
[30] Peter Harvey, *An Introduction to Buddhism: Teachings, History and Practices* (Cambridge: Cambridge Univ. Press, 2013), 285, 311, 429.
[31] Bhikkhu Bodhi, *The Numerical Discourses of the Buddha: A Translation of the Anguttara Nikaya* (Boston: Wisdom Publications, 2012), Book 8, section 51.
[32] Bodhi, Book 8, section 51.

that all men are created equal? It is because of the influence of Christianity throughout the modern world. Restated, it is because Christianity has shaped the modern world. Teaching that all people are created equal, and the stopping of *sati* noted below, are two examples of how Christians shape the world for Jesus Christ even apart from evangelism and discipleship. Having shown how worldviews differ, we will examine how shaping the world for Christ involves evangelism, discipleship, and much more.

Shaping the World for Christ

Faithful Christians try to shape the world for themselves but also try to shape the world for Christ. At the ultimate level, "shaping the world for Christ" means introducing an individual to the Christian faith in such a way that he or she eventually becomes a disciple. All Christians participate in God's work of shaping others' temporal and eternal destiny, and the arts can help reach that goal. This is the work of justification.

"Shaping the world for Christ" means building spiritual maturity in those who already know Jesus. By teaching truths, building communities, and shaping experiences, the arts can help current believers become more like Him. This is the work of sanctification.

Finally, "shaping the world for Christ" means influencing others with Christian thought and action, regardless of their religion or other belief systems. Indians used to practice *sati*, the self-immolation of widows on the funeral pyre of their husbands, in accordance with the traditional Hindu world view.[33] In Vedic teaching, Sati, the consort of the god Shiva, burned herself to death

---

[33] Ralph T H Griffith, Arthur Berriedale Keith, and Jon William Fergus, *The Vedas: The Saṃhitās of the Ṛig, Yajur (White and Black), Sāma, and Atharva Vedas* (United States: Kshetra Books, 2017), Rig Veda 10.18.7. *Atharva Veda*, Kanda 18, Sukta 3.

to preserve her honor after the humiliation of her husband. High born Hindu women were expected, and sometimes forced, to do the same.[34] The Christian world view of early 19th century Britain motivated the British, who controlled India, to forbid *sati*.[35] Even if the soldiers and officials of the East India Company were not themselves believers, the Christian worldview they inherited at home influenced them and the Hindus to end this tragic practice.

There are more examples of how promoting the Christian worldview, including through the arts, shapes the world for Christ. Key beliefs underpinning modern liberal democracy, such as the idea that all men are created equal, have a Judeo-Christian origin (Genesis 1-2, Leviticus 19:33-34, Psalms 67:4, Galatians 3:28).[36] Private property and markets are clearly part of the Biblical economy and are the foundation of capitalist economics (Exodus 20:15, 17, Deuteronomy 19:14, 27:17, Acts 4:36-5:11).[37] Individual liberty and free speech are pillars of Western thought that arise from the idea of the equality of all men (Genesis 1:26-28,

---

[34] A related suicidal Hindu practice was Jauhar, in which Hindu women immolated themselves en mass after military defeats.

[35] Rachel Fell Mcdermott et al., *Sources of Indian Traditions Modern India, Pakistan, and Bangladesh* (New York Chichester, West Sussex: Columbia University Press, 2014), 58.

[36] Some argue that the idea of human equality predated the Bible. This is false. Humans have been ranking themselves and others on a scale from demigods to subhumans since the beginning of history. Morality, freedom, and the protection of the environment are also Biblical concepts and have been since before time began (Genesis 1, 2).

[37] Capitalism is the primary Biblical economic system for nations. It is not untrammeled, however, as God instituted a safety net in the rules about gleaning (Leviticus 19:9-10), prohibition of usury (Exodus 22:25-27), the Sabbath day, the Sabbath year (Leviticus 25:1-7), and the income redistribution in the Jubilee year (Leviticus 25:8-17). Repeated warnings to care for the poor also factor into the Biblical safety net. Communism is not a Biblical economic system, but collective ownership of assets has occurred in specific, temporary, local settings in Church history (Acts 4:32-35). Shared ownership can constitute another brake on untrammeled capitalism and overbearing government.

Romans 3:23). Since all people are equal before their Creator, all people have equal rights before government.[38]

The arts are a powerful means to communicate a Christian worldview. Rembrandt's *The Return of the Prodigal Son*, drawn directly from a parable of Jesus, includes the repentant sinner, the sanctimonious older brother, and the grieved, later overjoyed, and all-forgiving father (Luke 15:11-32). Even for people who deny the name of Christ, Rembrandt (1606-1669) paints a profound human story of family rupture and restoration. Christian Christmas carols shape the thoughts of all those who sing or hear them, regardless of those peoples' stated beliefs. Bible poetry on walls, banners, and cards works magic even on those resistant to the message. One of the most secular organizations in the world, the United Nations, boasts a bronze sculpture entitled <u>Let Us Beat Our Swords into Ploughshares,</u> a direct quotation from Isaiah 2:4. The powerful effect of the Bible even on unbelievers is one reason many secularists are so opposed to crosses on steeples, verses on emails, and Bibles on desks. They hate and fear the power of the Word of God, so they vehemently deny of the validity of Scripture and vent venom or even violence on Christians.[39]

My prayer is that this book will encourage and empower pastors, other church leaders, artists, members of congregations,

---

[38] According to the Bible, all people are ultimately equal in four ways. First, we are all equal in being created. No human is self-existent, and no mortal is God. Second, every person is a sinner, a rebel against God. Third, all people are eligible for salvation through the work of Jesus Christ. Last, all people will be judged and rewarded or punished for what they do. The Creator does not value one creature over another. Beliefs in political equality derive from these foundational truths.

[39] Those who reject Christ are not wrong to hate and fear the word of God. Hebrews 4:12-13 reminds us "For the word of God is quick, and powerful, and sharper than any two-edged sword, piercing even to the dividing asunder of soul and spirit, and of the joints and marrow, and is a discerner of the thoughts and intents of the heart. Neither is there any creature that is not manifest in his sight: but all things are naked and opened unto the eyes of Him with whom we have to do." Christians do not need to weaponize the Bible...God already did it.

Shaping the World

and all other Christians, to use the arts to shape their churches, their communities, and their world for Jesus Christ.

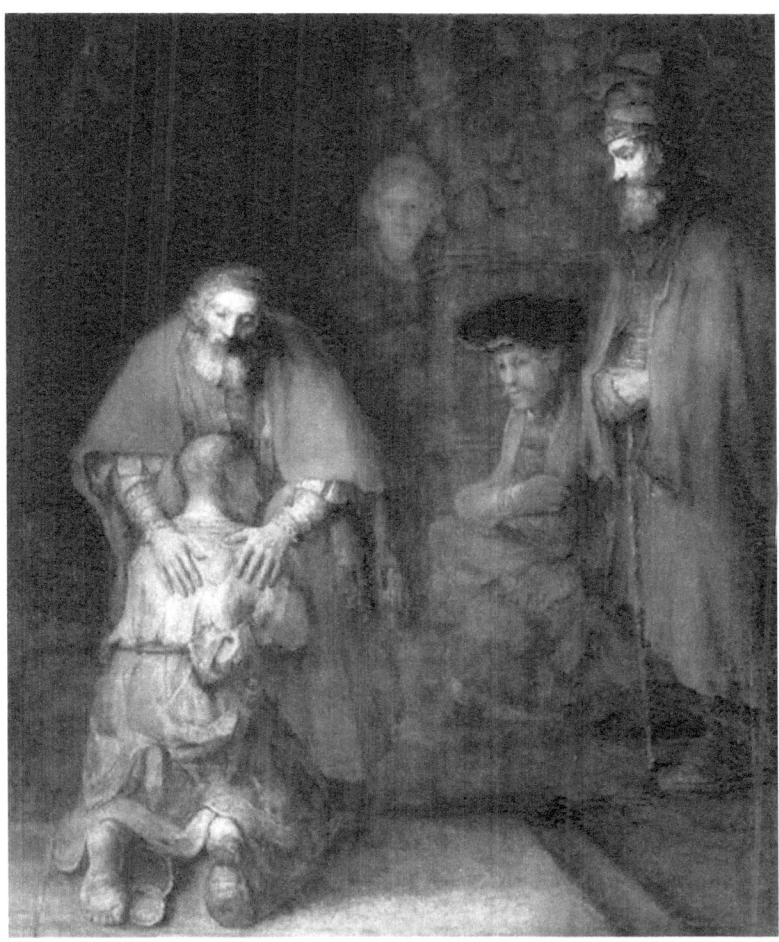

The State Hermitage Museum: Digital Collection, as Rembrandt, *Return of the Prodigal Son*, circa 1668[40]

---

[40] Rembrandt, *The Return of the Prodigal Son*, 1668, Oil on Canvas, 1668, Saint Petersburg, Hermitage Museum, https://upload.wikimedia.org/wikipedia/commons/9/93/Rembrandt_Harmensz_van_Rijn_-_Return_of_the_Prodigal_Son_-_Google_Art_Project.jpg.

Religion and Art

Discussion Questions for lessons, book, and Bible studies

1. Describe a time in your life in which you felt the grandeur of God through the medium of art.
2. Describe how you have used the arts to shape your world for personal reasons.
3. Share what arts you have participated in.
4. Describe how you have used the arts to shape your world for Christ.
5. Which of the arts is your favorite, and why?
6. Identify and explain how at least one non-Christian view, communicated through the arts, has shaped your life.
7. Identify and explain how at least one Christian view, communicated through the arts, has shaped your life.
8. What does the Bible say about the beliefs and actions noted in this chapter?

2

WHAT IS ART, AND WHAT ARE ITS CHARACTERISTICS, INCLUDING RELIGIOUS AND CHRISTIAN ART?

While objects like a tree can be clearly defined within and between cultures, concepts such as art defy definition. To many, art is "the quality, production, expression, or realm, according to aesthetic principles, of what is beautiful, appealing, or of more than ordinary significance."[41] This aesthetic focus may please a Westerner, but it may be unintelligible to someone from a culture that uses art as liturgy or for other purposes. Some Americans try to confine the use of art to contemplation, but for most of the world and in the truest sense, art acts.[42] Art is used to worship God, praise people (including defining who is considered "great" in each society), express emotion, communicate information, sell products, and make money.

Westerners historically differentiate between categories of art. In one scheme, works of fine (or high) art are enjoyed by the cultural elite in a society, works of popular art are shared broadly by the elite and the non-elite, and "works of the tribe" are shared by subgroups within a given society. Each individual may use art

---

[41] *Dictionary.com*, s.v. "Art," accessed March 9, 2016, http://www.dictionary.com/browse/art?s=t.
[42] Nicholas Wolterstorff, *Art in Action: Toward a Christian Aesthetic* (Grand Rapids: Eerdmans, 1987), 5.

in one or more of these categories. An unemployed single mother may only use popular art like television shows, movies, mainstream music, social media, and commercial visual arts such as magazine advertisements. A middle-class suburban Christian may enjoy not only such popular art but also Christian music and fiction (works of the tribe). A secular wealthy art collector with a passion for baseball may appreciate all three categories. Another version of this same idea is that fine art caters to the elite, popular art caters to the non-elite masses, and "works of the tribe" are shared by everyone in a society. Either way, Western conceptions of art differ.

This Western differentiation is foreign to many traditional cultures. In the Yakuma ritual, Sanni tribesmen of Sri Lanka use masks to heal disease. Diseases are thought to be caused by one or more of eighteen possible disease demons, and exorcists wear masks corresponding to the patient's specific symptom.[43] After the dance the disease-causing demon is driven out and the patient is thought to be healed. The masks are of the highest quality available in the culture and the ritual is common to every Sanni social group. The Papuan Gulf people of New Guinea use art in a similar healing ritual.[44] In these cases, as in most cultures, fine art, popular art and works of the tribe are the same.

---

[43] Mark S. Bailey and H. Janaka de Silva, "Sri Lankan Sanni Masks: An Ancient Classification of Disease," *British Medical Journal* 333.7582 (2006): 1327-28.
[44] Wolterstorff, 9-10.

What is Art?

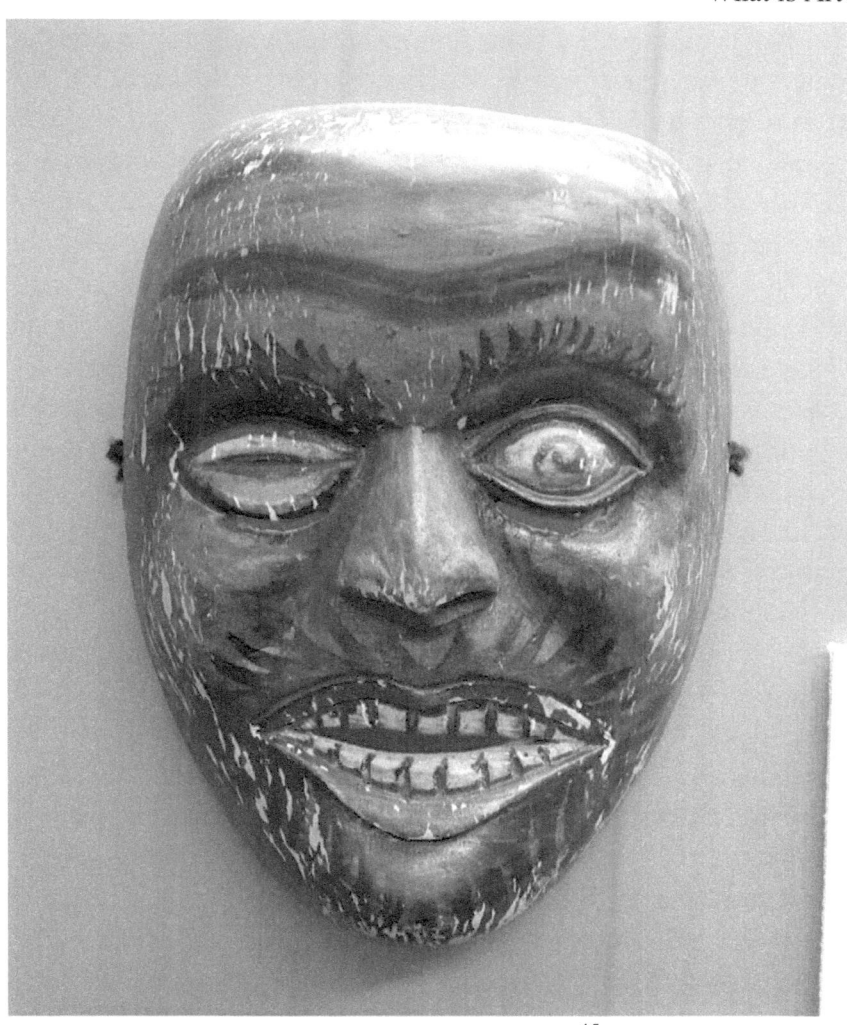

Sanni Mask of Sri Lanka[45]

---

[45] Kanna Sanni Yakka, Wood, Pigment, Montreal, Redpath Museum, accessed April 18, 2023, https://upload.wikimedia.org/wikipedia/commons/5/57/Kana_Sanni_Yakka_%28demon_of_blindness%29_mask%2C_Sri_Lanka%2C_19th-20th_century%2C_wood%2C_pigment_-_Redpath_Museum_-_McGill_University_-_Montreal%2C_Canada_-_DSC08189.jpg.

Religion and Art

Now that people from Anchorage to Zurich can tour the Louvre or see a rock concert on their smart phones, almost all types of art are available to nearly anyone at any time. As a result, the distinctions between fine art, popular art, and works of the tribe are fading. Simultaneously, other divisions have arisen, especially generational and cultural. Young Hispanics listen to radio and television, read books, watch movies, and attend religious services, produced by and for young Hispanics. Members of other economic classes, generations and cultural groups do the same. People remain within their group, rarely experiencing, much less enjoying, anything outside.[46] Art has splintered just like food, education, and so many things in the modern world. Art has also flattened, becoming more homogeneous, and many would argue, lower quality. For example, Western pop music in the 2010s had less variation in pitch transitions, homogenization of the timbral palette, more loudness, and poorer volume dynamics than popular music fifty years ago.[47]

Many Christians eschew the arts altogether. Even Christians who appreciate art often find themselves culturally in a "Christian ghetto", experiencing only Christian-themed music, paintings, and other art works, and experiencing these only with other Christians. By limiting themselves to Christian themed art, they make themselves incapable of learning from and commenting on secular works and thereby limit their impact on the wider world. Simultaneously, such people protect themselves from ideas that may create stress, provide temptation, and challenge their Christian faith.

Artists who follow Christ sometimes only produce art for other believers. While doing so avoids the scrutiny of non-

---

[46] William A. Dyrness, *Visual Faith: Art, Theology, and Worship in Dialogue* (Grand Rapids: Baker Academic, 2001), 15.

[47] Joan Serrà et al., "Measuring the Evolution of Contemporary Western Popular Music," *Scientific Reports* 2, no. 1 (July 26, 2012), https://doi.org/10.1038/srep00521.

Christian eyes, it also prevents constructive feedback from non-Christian tongues. Worse, it avoids impacting secular hearts. Christian arts fans and artists who stay in a "Christian bubble" limit their artistic impact on the larger society.

Art is universal; there is no country or culture in the world, or in history, that does not have music, fiction, poetry, sculpture, painting (at least calligraphy), and other art forms.[48] It is hard to find someone who experiences no art at all.

Key Characteristics of Art

Francis Schaeffer's (1912-1984) essay *Some Perspectives on Art* outlines more key characteristics. First, he notes that art has value in and of itself, regardless of the truth or falsehood of the worldview portrayed therein.[49] The simple fact that an artist, a person made in the image of God, created a piece of art, regardless of how beautiful or ugly others consider it to be, confers value upon that art. Art is more than the embodiment of a message, it is the embodiment of part of a person. Since that person has intrinsic value, the art that he or she creates has intrinsic value. Second, art adds power to the world view that it communicates, regardless of the content or truth of that world view.[50] Consider the command "Thou shalt not kill (Exodus 20:13)." The sentence has implicit power to prevent murder, but that power is multiplied when Shakespeare makes the same point in *Macbeth*.

Third, Schaeffer argues that art should be judged by four standards: technical excellence, validity, intellectual content, and integration of content and vehicle.[51] *Technical excellence* refers to how skillfully the artist works in his or her medium. Musicians

---

[48] Wolterstorff, 4.
[49] Francis A. Schaeffer, *Art and the Bible* (Downers Grove, Ill.: IVP Books, 2006), 50.
[50] Schaeffer, 57.
[51] Schaeffer, 62.

producing a clear tone with good rhythm and dynamics may be technically excellent. *Validity* refers to whether a piece of art honestly reflects the character and worldview of the artist. Martin Luther King Jr's (1929-1968) speech *I Have a Dream* was valid because it reflected who he was. The same speech given by George Wallace (1919-1998), the segregationist governor of Alabama, would have been ridiculous. *Intellectual content* is about the message of the art, and how accurately it reflects objective reality (reality as it appears to God, as revealed in the created order and the Bible). *Integration of content and vehicle* asks if the message of a piece of art matches the delivery of the piece. Television, for example, is not a good vehicle to communicate complex ideas, but is excellent for simple ideas in video clips and sound bites. The Lincoln-Douglas US Senate debates (1858) would have flopped on television, but *The Simpsons*, an off-color parody of American life, thrived.

    Fourth, art can examine and enrich any message, from fantasy to history or science.[52] No style of art is inherently good or evil. Marshall McLuhan (1911-1980) was partially accurate when he said that "the medium is the message," but the medium (style of art) cannot make a good message evil or an evil message good.[53] The German slogan *Arbeit macht frei* was placed on the gates of Nazi concentration camps in World War 2.[54] The context made this simple slogan evil, even though the medium, a sign on a gate, was not. By contrast, the Bible contains many examples of God sending His messages, inherently good by virtue of His perfect character, by a variety of means. Bezalel built, David sang, and Ezekiel

---

[52] Schaeffer, 71.
[53] Eric McLuhan, "Commonly Asked Questions (and Answers)," Marshall McLuhan, accessed July 14, 2016, https://www.marshallmcluhan.com/common-questions/.
[54] "Work makes free," which was a cruel lie to inmates almost guaranteed to starve, suffer, and die, no matter what they did.

dramatized - visual, musical, and the performing arts were all part of the Lord's tidings to His people.

Another example of the four criteria used to judge the value of art may be useful. Imagine that a Muslim man named Ahmed wants to tell the world about Islam by putting a bumper sticker on his car. He makes a white sticker, 11" x 3" rectangle, with the *Shahada* ("there is no God but Allah, and Mohammad is His prophet") printed on it in black block letters. Meanwhile, a Christian man named John wants to tell the world about Jesus by putting a bumper sticker on his car. He makes a white sticker, 11" x 3" rectangle, with John 3:16 ("For God so loved the world that he gave his one and only Son, that whoever believes in him shall not perish but have eternal life.") printed on it in black block letters. Both bumper stickers are in English and are alike in every other way. How do we judge the art value of these bumper stickers?

From a technical quality standpoint, they are the same; uninspired but functional. A Muslim would rate the content of the *Shahada* sticker higher, and a Christian would rate the content of the John 3:16 sticker higher. Both stickers are equally valid in that they accurately reflect the beliefs of the person who displayed them. From the standpoint of the vehicle matching the message, however, Ahmed's bumper sticker is better. The *Shahada* is shorter, fits better on a bumper sticker, and therefore the lettering can be larger and easier to read from a distance than John 3:16.

Schaeffer's perspective on the key characteristics of art is enlightening, but is limited to his knowledge and experience of art. Other critics may come up with a different set of characteristics based on their knowledge and experience. However, all commentators base their opinions on a review of extant art because it is difficult to comment on something that does not exist. This fact makes patronage, the support given by a patron to an artist, extremely important. Without a patron to provide resources, artists are often unable to make art. Art that doesn't exist, because the artist did not have a patron, cannot be critiqued. Since patrons often decide what they want artists to make, patronage heavily influences what art gets produced.

The Church was once the greatest patron of the arts in Europe.[55,56] In the Middle Ages (500s-1300s) and Renaissance (1300s-1600s), the Church and wealthy individuals sponsored artists to produce art for pedagogy, prestige, pleasure, and profit.[57] Pope Julius II (1443-1513) ordered the rebuilding of Saint Peter's Basilica and commissioned Michelangelo (1475-1564) to paint a fresco on the ceiling of the Sistine Chapel.[58] In the Modern Era (1700-1950), governments, large philanthropic organizations, and individuals commission arts. The early American painter Gilbert Stewart (1755-1828) produced portraits of the first six Presidents of the United States, as well as celebrities from John Jacob Astor (1763-1848) to Martha Washington (1731-1802). Today commercial interests sponsor a wide variety of art. For example, the global accounting firm Ernst and Young sponsored the exhibition *Monet in the 20th Century* at the Royal Academy of the Arts in London,[59] while the Dutch company, Shell Oil, has funded art festivals in Ireland.[60]

---

[55] Schafer, 17.

[56] J Scott McElroy, *Creative Church Handbook: Releasing the Power of the Arts in Your Congregation* (Downers Grove, IL: InterVarsity Press, 2015), 259.

[57] Use of money for building or art, as opposed to giving money to the poor, has been reviled in certain circles since Judas Iscariot (John 12:5-6). Such accusations may or may not be valid. The poor benefit from beauty at least as much as the rich, who have more of it. The church may have been the most beautiful thing in the lives of paupers.

[58] Terry Glaspey, *75 Masterpieces Every Christian Should Know: the Fascinating Stories Behind Great Works of Art, Literature, Music, and Film* (Grand Rapids: Baker Books, 2015), 69-73.

[59] Emma Clark, "The Art of Sponsorship," *BBC News*, August 17, 2001, accessed March 9, 2016, http://news.bbc.co.uk/2/hi/business/1494482.stm.

[60] Mark Brown and Terry Macalister, "Oil Companies' Sponsorship of the Arts 'is Cynical PR Strategy'," *Guardian*, April 19, 2015, accessed March 9, 2016,

Unexpected Arts

Most people include painting, sculpture, music, dance, drama, poetry, literature, and similar activities under the heading "the arts." Everyone eats food and wears clothes, but few include culinary and fashion when they think of "the arts." Culinary and fashion mix necessity and aesthetics. They have been used in every era to shape the world for Jesus Christ. Culinary artists harmonize taste, scent, texture, and the appearance of food to provide not only nourishing, healthy, and delicious dishes but a unique sensory (visual, tactile, olfactory, gustatory, and sometimes even auditory) experience. An army nurse that I once knew was also a gourmet chef. He invited friends and superiors to his home for marvelous meals and colorful conversation. His talents gave him the ear of many an influential leader.

Christian families sometimes make "Resurrection rolls" at Easter. The marshmallow represents the body of Christ, the dough represents His grave wrappings, and the oven represents His tomb. The baker dips the marshmallow into butter and cinnamon-sugar, representing the preparation of Jesus' body with oil and spices. The baker then wraps the marshmallow (the body) tightly with the dough (the grave wrappings) and puts the roll into the oven (the tomb). When the Resurrection roll is baked, it is pulled out of the oven (the tomb). Then the roll (the grave clothes) is opened, and the marshmallow (the body of Jesus) is gone. Mothers have long used Resurrection rolls to teach children about the crucifixion, burial, and resurrection of the Lord. Hot Cross Buns mark the end of the Lenten season with a cross, spices, and orange peel to commemorate His suffering and death. Santa Lucia bread (Saffron buns) reflects the historical persecution of Christians and anticipate

---

http://www.theguardian.com/environment/2015/apr/19/oil-companies-arts-sponsorship-cynical-pr-strategy-says-activist.

Religion and Art

Jesus' coming and saving work at Christmas. All are examples of using culinary arts to shape the world for Christ.

Resurrection Rolls Recipe[61]

> Prep Time - 10 minutes
> Cook Time - 15 minutes
> Total Time - 25 minutes
> Servings - 8
> Calories - 99 kcal

Ingredients
- 1 x 10 ounce can refrigerated crescent dinner rolls
- 8 large marshmallows
- 1/4 cup butter, melted
- 2 teaspoons cinnamon
- 1/4 cup sugar

Instructions

Preheat the oven to 350°F. Line a baking sheet with a parchment or silicone liner. Open the crescent roll package and separate the rolls into eight triangles.
In a small bowl, whisk together the cinnamon and sugar. Dip each of the marshmallows in the melted butter, then roll in the cinnamon sugar mixture.
Place a marshmallow in the middle of each dough triangle, then roll the dough tightly around the marshmallow, pinching to close all of the seams.
Place the rolls on the prepared baking sheet. Bake for 10-14 minutes, or until golden brown.

---

[61] Kristyn Merkley, "Resurrection Rolls," *Lil' Luna* (blog), March 9, 2023, https://lilluna.com/resurrection-rolls/.

What is Art?

Fashion arts are more than merely buying and wearing clothes. They use design, color, texture, and fabric to provide comfortable, attractive, functional, and meaningful garments, footwear, headwear, and accessories. Fashion provides a fascinating window into every society, including climate, work, gender expectations, and wealth. As revealed in such period works such as Jane Austin's *Pride and Prejudice*, wealthy and middle-class men in early 19th century England wore top hats, impractical for most activities but intended to confer authority. Similarly placed women wore dresses, ornamented according to their status. Wearing clothes slightly beyond one's station is a time-honored technique to "move up in the world." People do the same with houses (architecture) and conveyances (vehicle design). In *Pride and Prejudice*, Lady Catherine De Bourgh's carriage is ornate, as she wishes to display her wealth, taste, and power. Mr. Bennet's carriage is ordinary, as he can't afford anything more.

My wife, daughters, and many friends have told me how hard it is to find modest, high quality, and attractive women's clothes. Additionally, women's clothes often don't have pockets or anything to hold a wallet or a cell phone. Presumably this is because our society, like every other society in history, values beauty over practicality for its female members. How wonderful it would be if talented Christian fashion designers could combine modesty, beauty, and practicality in women's clothing! After all, God Himself identified the importance of clothing in His service. The garments of the Hebrew high priest communicated God's beauty, creativity, power, authority, and attention to detail (Exodus 28).

In *The Hidden Art of Homemaking*, Edith Schaeffer (1914-2013), widow of Christian philosopher Francis Schaffer, describes scores of ways to bring art into everyday life.[62] Far from being a

---

[62] Edith Schaeffer, The Hidden Art of Homemaking, Creative Ideas for Enriching Everyday Life, (London, Tyndale House, 1971).

drudgery of dishes and dusting, homemaking can include painting, sculpture, gardening, flower arranging, and creative recreation. Beautiful touches for the home can be made for very little money. The only real limit is one's creativity.

Religious and Christian Art

Just as it is difficult to define art, so it is challenging to define Christian art. Some may consider Christian art to be art produced by professed Christians, others may opine that it is art with Biblical or Christian themes, while a few may think that it is art created for a Christian audience. We will use all three definitions. A broader perspective is to define Christian art as art which reveals God in a way consistent with Christian theology, regardless of the beliefs of the artist, the theme of the piece, or the characteristics of the audience. Such classic works as Picasso's *Guernica* and Henry Moore's *Mother and Child*, both of which have powerful spiritual overtones, could then be included.[63] I invite the reader to decide which definition is best in his or her life and ministry context.

Christian art was the primary art in Europe until the Renaissance and featured such masterpieces as Leonardo da Vinci's (1452-1519) *Last Supper*, Raphael's (1483-1520) *Deposition of Christ*, and Handel's (1685-1759) *Messiah*. Other examples include the Cathedral at Chartres (1134), and the *Book of Kells*, an illuminated manuscript of the Gospels from the Kells Monastery near Dublin (c 550).

Christian art had many purposes beyond aesthetic contemplation. The Anglican Reverend Regan O' Callaghan wrote "Icons have many functions across different traditions. They enhance the beauty of a church and instruct the faithful. They

---

[63] Michelle P. Brown, *The Lion Companion to Christian Art* (Oxford: Lion Hudson, 2008), 14.

illustrate the sacred scriptures. They serve as reminders of Christ's crucifixion, his death and suffering. The icon as an aid for prayer can be part of the whole experience of the Eucharist and liturgy."[54] What applies to icons applies to other types of Christian art.

As discussed earlier, people use everything they have to shape the world to their liking. They use the tools at their disposal, whether a stethoscope for a physician, a rifle for a soldier, or a paint brush for an artist. Artists make art to sustain themselves, achieve fame, fulfill personal needs, or to advance an agenda. Usually, they ply their trade for a combination of these reasons. But even if they don't realize it, every piece of art communicates a point of view. No one, whether engineer, priest, or artist, can separate themselves from their work. A Muslim artist will communicate Islam in his poetry even if he does not intend to. The same is true for a Hindu, Buddhist, Jew, or Christian. C.S. Lewis recognized this when he said, "I believe in Christianity as I believe that the sun has risen, not only because I see it, but because by it I see everything else."[65] A devout Muslim may say the same thing about Islam, a secularist about humanism, or anyone else about their belief system. People shape the world in ways that they understand and intend, and in ways that they don't. The only way for Christians not to use the arts to shape the world is for them to not produce or consume art at all.

---

[64] Revd. Regan O' Callaghan, quoted in Michelle Brown, *The Lion Companion to Christian Art* (Oxford: Lion, 2008), 94.
[65] "A Quote by C.S. Lewis," www.goodreads.com, accessed May 30, 2023, https://www.goodreads.com/quotes/660-i-believe-in-christianity-as-i-believe-that-the-sun.

Religion and Art

Discussion Questions for lessons, book, and Bible studies

1. How do you define and categorize art?
2. Identify and explain the key characteristics of art.
3. Describe some unexpected arts in your life.
4. How do you define Christian art?
5. How could you make food and clothing a form of art in your family, church, and community?
6. How could you make other everyday activities into art forms to communicate Jesus Christ and bless your family, church, and community?
7. What does the Bible say about the beliefs and actions noted in this chapter?

3

OVERVIEW OF MAJOR RELIGIONS AND PHILOSOPHIES

Before we learn how Christians have used art to shape the world for Christ, and can do so in the future, let us examine some other religions and philosophies and see how their members use the arts to shape their environment. We live in a multicultural, pluralistic world. Islam, Hinduism, Buddhism, other faiths, political activism of various varieties, and secular humanism (with its equally materialistic counterparts) are competitors to Christianity in the marketplace of ideas. Christians must be aware of how non-Christians use the arts to accomplish their purposes, which often directly oppose ours. The Great Commission (Matthew 28:18-20) compels disciples of Christ to love those who do not know Him, to speak to them in ways that they can understand, and in so doing to introduce them to the Lord who lived, died, and rose again for them.

Christianity is a religion and way of life. To be a Christian, one must "believe on the Lord Jesus Christ, and thou shalt be saved" (Acts 16:31). This dogma is key to the faith, although Christianity is far more than a single statement. Followers of Jesus consider the Bible to be authoritative over their lives.

The New Testament has no instructions for building a "Christian" government or political system. It does not tell us what kings, princes, prime ministers, or presidents must do, except for the general injunctions to trust God and rule righteously. The Old

Testament instructions for building Israel into a political nation do not apply to followers of Christ today, although they are useful to inform government in any age.

Jesus was never a secular ruler and never led an army. Instead, Jesus taught "my kingdom is not of this world" (John 18:36). He encouraged the rich, poor, powerful, and weak to follow Him, and did so equally. Paul designed the local church but the only thing that he had to say about the local magistrate was that Christians should obey him (Romans 13).[66] Although the Christian world view heavily influences temporal government, the political aspects that have accreted on to Christianity since Constantine (272-337) are not organic to the faith.

Islam

In pre-Islamic Arabia, Arabs were non-sedentary (Bedouins) or sedentary (city dwelling). Mecca was a trading city administered by the sedentary Arab Quraysh tribe, who claimed to be of the bloodline of Abraham.[67] Tribesmen were custodians of the Kabah, an ancient place of Arabic polytheistic worship. Worship practices including walking around the Kabah (circumambulation), pilgrimage to Mecca, animal sacrifice, use of amulets, following omens, astrology, and divination (often by the casting of arrows).

Mohammad ibn Abdullah (570-632) was born to a Quraysh family. His father died a few months before his birth and his

---

[66] Christian obedience to secular authorities applies in almost every situation. The only exception is when those authorities directly oppose the teachings or the spirit of the teachings of God (Acts 5:29). Also, in governments such as democracies when Christians become the magistrates, these Christians are constrained by the teachings of Scripture.

[67] Raana Bokhari et al., *The Illustrated Encyclopedia of Islam: A Comprehensive Guide to the History, Philosophy and Practice of Islam around the World, with More than 500 Beautiful Illustrations* (London: Lorenz Books, 2009), 14-15.

mother died when he was six. Mohammad's uncle Abu Talib, a rich merchant and experienced caravan handler, took him in. At age 25, Mohammad married a wealthy caravan businesswoman named Khadijah (555-619), providing more opportunities to learn business, trade, and negotiations...skills that would serve him well in the future.

Mohammad's first vision of the angel Jibril (Gabriel) was in 610. Over the next 12 years, he was reputed to have received more visions and shared them with his family and friends. Slowly, many came to believe him and become Muslims. Persecution from the polytheistic Quraysh increased, and in 622 he and his followers fled to Medina in what Muslims famously know as the *Hijra* (migration). For the next eight years, Mohammad and his Muslim band fought the Quraysh, finally taking Mecca in 630 and converting them to Islam. Mohammad's Muslim forces attacked other tribes to compel them to join him, and he began military expeditions against Byzantium and Persia before his death in 632. Mohammad had many wives, including the nine-year-old Aisha. He had no sons.

Abu Bakir (573-634), first of the Rashidun (rightly guided) caliphs took power in 632. Under his leadership, Muslim gained control of the entire Arabian Peninsula and attacked Byzantium and Persia. Umar ibn al-Khaṭṭāb (582-644), the second Rashid, crushed the Byzantines at Yarmuk (636), destroyed the Persians at Qadisya (636) and Nahavand (642), and conquered Egypt (641). He led the faithful through the bubonic plague epidemic of 638). Uthman ibn Affan (573-656) followed, finishing off Persia and conquering North Africa. Alī ibn Abī Ṭālib (632-661) was the last of the Rashidun, presiding over the first Muslim civil war (656-661).

The Islamic Empires included the Umayyads (661-750, Abbasids (750-1258), Fatimids (909-1171), Seljuks (1104-1308), Safavids (1501-1736), Moors (711-1453), Mughals (1526-1857), and Ottomans (1299-1922). Between them, Islam controlled space and people more than double what the Roman Empire ever knew.

Islam is a religion, a way of life, and a political system. To be a Muslim, one must affirm "there is no god but *Allah*, and Mohammad is his prophet" (*Shahada*). Muslims must also do good works involving the other pillars of Islam, which include daily prayers (*Salat*), paying taxes (*Zakat*), fasting, especially at Ramadan (*Sa'am*), and the pilgrimage to Mecca (*Hajj*). Traditionally, Muslims consider the *Sharia*, including the *Quran*, the *Sunna* (the part of Muslim law based on the *Hadiths*, words, and acts of Mohammad), and *fiqh* (Islamic jurisprudence), to be authoritative over their lives.

Consistent with the temporal nature of Islam, the *Sharia* contains specific instructions in governance. Caliphs are to lead the Faithful (*umma* or Muslim community) politically as well as religiously.[68] Mohammad was a religious leader and a head of state. He was a warrior who led armies and conquered foes. His vision was that every nation and people would embrace Islam, and thereby *Allah* would bring justice to the world. While Islam teaches its own version of paradise for individuals after death, the victory of *Allah* was to be an earthly one. The peace trumpeted by apologists for Islam is traditionally focused on the justice and well-being that all mankind will enjoy once everyone is submitted to *Allah* and every nation falls under the supremacy of Islam.[69] Restated, when Islamic texts talk of peace, they mean the peace that will occur once every person, or at least every nation, is Muslim.

Today, Islam is the second largest religion in the world, with 1.4 billion self-proclaimed adherents. The vast majority of

---

[68] Ahmad Naqib al-Misri, *The Reliance of the Traveller* (Beltsville MD: Amana Publications, 1991), O25.0, 638-648.
[69] Majid Khadduri, *The Islamic Conception of Justice* (Baltimore: Johns Hopkins University Press, 2003), 163-171.

world Muslims live in the triangle from Senegal to Kazakhstan to Indonesia.[70] Due to higher birth rates, Islam is projected to be the fastest growing religion in the world through 2050.[71] Muslims comprised 23.2% of the global population in 2010, but Muslims are expected to increase to 29.7% by 2050.

Hinduism

Hinduism has no known founder, but its adherents prefer to think that Hindu religious truths simply evolved out of the distant past. In the second millennium BC, Aryan peoples from Central Asia moved into the Indian subcontinent and recorded their beliefs into the Vedas, the holiest scriptures of Hinduism. Under the influence of Buddhism, Jainism, and other religious and cultural traditions, scholars of the Vedic religion wrote the Upanishads. These books moved Indians from a more ritual based Brahmanism to a more philosophical early Hinduism. Under the influence of Christianity, Hindu scholars wrote the Bhagavad Gita (1st century AD). The combination of these forces, and 2000 years of history, have shaped Hinduism into what it is today.

Unlike Christianity, Islam, and Judaism, in which the written word is preeminent, Hinduism is a visual religion. A Hindu will not go to a temple to "worship" but to "see" the deity.[72] The gaze of a deity as found in an idol, the sight of a sacred place, or the gaze of a famous religious leader, which is known as *Darsan*,

---

[70] World Population Review, "Muslim Population by Country 2023," worldpopulationreview.com, 2023, https://worldpopulationreview.com/country-rankings/muslim-population-by-country.

[71] Pew Research Center, "Key Findings from the Global Religious Futures Project," *Pew Research Center*, December 21, 2022, https://www.pewresearch.org/religion/2022/12/21/key-findings-from-the-global-religious-futures-project/.

[72] Diana L. Eck, *Darśan: Seeing the Divine Image in India*, 3rd ed. (New York: Columbia University Press, 1998), 3.

is imbued with power to bless.[73] Similarly, the "evil eye" of an enemy has power to curse.[74] Seeing is a kind of touching. Hence the visual arts are integral to Hinduism.

Hinduism is a religion, a way of life, and a political system. Adherents share foundational principles, such as the *Brahman* (the universal spirit), *samsara* (the cycle of life, death, and rebirth), *moksha* (deliverance from samsara and entry into eternal bliss), *dharma* (duty to do good works, teaching, righteousness), and *kharma* (cause and effect of works done). Hindus may worship many different gods (polytheism), may believe that everything is god (pantheism), believe that there is only one god (monotheism), or believe in no gods (atheism).[75]

Hindu scriptures, including the *sruti* (revealed) and *smrti* (remembered) texts do not have the same authority over Hindus that the Abrahamic texts (*Tanakh*, Bible, *Quran*) have over followers of the Abrahamic religions. Adherents are freer to choose which texts to believe and how to believe them, disregarding texts or the interpretations of texts, within broad limits, as it suits them. Hindus are distinguished more by their actions (orthopraxy) rather than their beliefs (orthodoxy). The fundamental tenets of Hinduism include caste and rebirth.[76]

Guidance on governance is found throughout Hindu scriptures. The traditional caste system is a social and political construct found in the holiest of *sruti*, including *Brahmins* (religious leaders), *Kshatriya* (warriors, administrators), *Vaishya* (merchants, landowners), *Shudra* (commoners, peasants, and servants), and *Dalits* (separated, untouchables, out of the caste system). The *Laws of Manu* is a *smrti* legal text touching on every part of Indian life. In works such as the *Arthashastra*, Hinduism as

---

[73] Darsan is literally sight or vision in Sanskrit.
[74] Eck, 7.
[75] R C Zaehner, *Hinduism* (New York: Oxford Paperbacks, 1966), 1-2.
[76] Zaehner, 4, 8.

written has much to say about temporal rule. Historically, there is no differentiation of the "religious" and "secular" realms in Indian languages.

Hindus comprised 15% of the global population in 2010, a number which is expected to be about the same in 2050.[77] Hindus are concentrated in India and Nepal, with tiny populations in the rest of the world. Hinduism is not a missionary religion, as Christianity is. Hinduism is less a militant religion than Islam. Rather, Hinduism is mainly an ethnic religion.

Buddhism

Siddhartha Gautama (560-480 BC) was a prince of the Kingdom of Sakya, near modern Nepal.[78] His father was King Suddhodana and his mother Queen Maya, but she died shortly after Siddhartha's birth. He was being groomed to take the throne, as was his duty in life. In his twenties, Gautama married Yasodhara, and the couple had a son, Rāhula. Over time, Siddhartha discovered suffering and death in life, renounced his birthright, and became a wandering ascetic. He later disavowed asceticism, after his "enlightment," preached a "Middle Path" between indulgence and asceticism. The Buddha established a monastic community, the Sangha, and a lay community. He did not participate in war but did collaborate with rulers who did. Siddhartha Gautama died in 480 BC. His wife became a Buddhist nun and his son a Buddhist monk.

Buddhism is a 6th century BC offshoot of Hinduism and holds similar views regarding *samsara*, *moksha*, *karma*, *dharma*, and the like. The Buddha (Siddhartha Gautama) taught the Four

---

[77] Pew Research Center, "Key Findings from the Global Religious Futures Project," *Pew Research Center*, December 21, 2022, https://www.pewresearch.org/religion/2022/12/21/key-findings-from-the-global-religious-futures-project/.
[78] Reliable sources about the life of the Buddha are few, so his story must be considered semi-legendary.

Noble Truths:[79] (1) everything is suffering, (2) craving causes suffering, (3) to extinguish suffering, extinguish craving, and (4) the path leading to the extinction of suffering includes the right view (knowledge of suffering), right resolve (live rightly), right speech, right action (avoid murder, theft, and sexual excess), right livelihood (avoiding occupations that harm or torment other beings – butchers, hunters, brewers, thieves, prostitutes),[80] right effort, right mindfulness (conscious control of body), and right concentration (turn away from the world).

Buddhism is a religion and a way of life, but it also has something to say about temporal affairs. The Buddha ordered his monks to obey the king and forbade them from political activity. He sought the support of kings and actively collaborated with them, even to the point of accepting royal spies among his monks.[81] Gautama did not include the soldiery in the list of proscribed occupations under "right livelihood." To do so would have alienated the monarchs whose support he sought. The Buddha was the chief administrator of the Buddhist order, including all monks, monasteries, and lay members. The *Vinaya Pitaka* (Basket of Discipline) comprised the rules for the Monastic Order (*Sangha*).[82] Other parts of the *Pali Canon*, known as the *Tipitaka* and honored in the Theravada and Mahayana traditions, include the *Sutta Pitaka* and the *Abhidhamma Pitaka*.[83] Mahayana Buddhism also reveres many sutras as scripture, including the Lotus sutra, Heart sutra, and Diamond sutra.

---

[79] Hans Wolfgang Schumann, *The Historical Buddha: The Times, Life, and Teachings of the Founder of Buddhism* (London: Arkana, 1989), 64-65.
[80] Schumann, 148.
[81] Schumann, 117-119.
[82] Ainslie Embree and Stephen Hay, eds., *Sources of Indian Tradition.*, 2nd ed., vol. 1, From the Beginning to 1800 (Introduction to Oriental Civilizations) (New York: Columbia University Press, 1988), 99.
[83] Harvey, 459.

Overview of Major Religions

Buddhists comprised 7.1% of the world's population in 2010, but that number is expected to decline to 5.2% by 2050.[84] Though Buddhism is a missionary religion in a way that Hinduism is not, Buddhist majority nations such as Japan have some of the lowest fertility rates in the world, not even meeting replacement.

As of 2020, 57 countries had a state religion, a number which has increased from 40 in 2007. Countries with state religions had the highest number of government restrictions on religion. 63% of countries with a state religion were Islamic.[85]

Secular Humanism, Marxism, and Critical Theory

Secular humanism denies being a religion but has many of the characteristics of religion, as shown in Table 7 of Appendix 1. It denies any reality outside the material world and rejects the existence of transcendent right and wrong (good and evil), apart from what the consensus of humanity (or at least an individual culture) believes. In secular humanism, there is no soul, no salvation, and no afterlife.

Pastor and US Senator Raphael Warnock captured the essence of humanism when he wrote, "The meaning of Easter is more transcendent than the resurrection of Jesus Christ. Whether you are Christian or not, through a commitment to helping others we are able to save ourselves."[86] In this view, religion

---

[84] Pew Research Center, "Key Findings from the Global Religious Futures Project," Pew Research Center, December 21, 2022, https://www.pewresearch.org/religion/2022/12/21/key-findings-from-the-global-religious-futures-project/.

[85] Pew Research Center, "Key Findings from the Global Religious Futures Project," Pew Research Center, December 21, 2022, https://www.pewresearch.org/religion/2022/12/21/key-findings-from-the-global-religious-futures-project/.

[86] Michelle Borstein, "Sen. Raphael Warnock's Deleted Easter Tweet Reflects Religious and Political Chasms about Christianity," *Washington Post*, April 5,

(Christianity) is unnecessary and probably unhelpful. To secular humanists, assisting others on this earth in this life is the only real salvation, because there is no life hereafter. Jesus' teaching that we should focus on earthly life primarily as it relates to eternity (Matthew 10:28) has no place in secular humanism, which rejects eternity and life after death.

Secular humanism began with a modernist paradigm, arguing that representative democracy, science, the victory of "reason" over "superstition," a secular metanarrative, continuous human progress, and technology would save the world.[87] The carnage of the world wars, the threat of nuclear annihilation, and a loss of confidence in the Western world ushered in a new paradigm, postmodernism. In postmodern thought, there is no overarching story for human existence (no "metanarrative"), such as the Christian salvation story or the modernist belief in perpetual secular progress. All truth claims are suspect or even invalid, and power is all that matters. What a speaker or writer means is irrelevant compared to what the hearer or reader understands in the message. Life is a zero-sum game between individuals and groups, has no inherent meaning (aside from what each person or group puts into it), has no objective morals, and is completely defined by what individuals or their communities wish to make it.

In modern philosophy, Marxism is a common bedfellow with secular humanism. Karl Marx argued that life is fundamentally a struggle between holders of capital (money in its various forms) and non-holders of capital. The former, labeled bourgeoisie, are those who own a means of production, such as property or a factory. The latter, labeled proletariat, are those who do not own a means of production but instead are required to work

---

2021, https://www.washingtonpost.com/religion/2021/04/05/raphael-warnock-deletes-tweet-easter-resurrection-jeremiah-wright/.

[87] Helen Pluckrose and James Lindsay, *Cynical Theories: How Activist Scholarship Made Everything about Race, Gender, and Identity-and Why This Harms Everybody* (Durham, North Carolina: Pitchstone Publishing, 2020), 11.

Overview of Major Religions

for a living. Proletarians include anyone who works for a wage, from street sweepers to physicians.

Marx opposed religion, as he believed that nothing existed beyond the physical universe. To him, religion was the opiate of the masses, a technique used by the oppressors (bourgeoisie) to give the oppressed (proletarians) a little comfort in their lifelong misery. Such would delay the revolution of the oppressed against their overlords.

Critical theory includes such philosophical movements as post-colonialism, feminism, queer studies, disability and fat studies, and critical race theory. Critical theories describe reality by combining a postmodern framework of universal and extreme cynicism about Truth with a neo-Marxist framework of perceived power imbalances and perpetual conflict.[88] Two key postmodern principles are at work:[89]

1. Knowledge – objective knowledge either does not exist or is not obtainable due to mankind's inherent biases and power dynamics. Knowledge is culturally constructed.
2. Politics – societies are formed by systems of hierarchy and power. These systems decide what can be known.

Major themes in postmodern also come into play in the various critical theories.[90]

1. Boundaries are blurred. For example, sex is not binary (male and female) but a continuum. Races do not exist. Putting anything into categories, such as is required in science, is oppressive. Science as we know it is Western and oppressive.

---

[88] Pluckrose and Lindsay, 98.
[89] Pluckrose and Lindsay, 31.
[90] Pluckrose and Lindsay, 31.

2. Language has the power to create "reality." Therefore, it must be controlled. Free speech is oppressive.
3. Cultures are relative. They are all constructed, and none is better than another.
4. The universal does not exist, as nothing is true for everyone. Furthermore, the individual does not exist. Each person is a combination of the groups that he or she is in...nothing more.

For feminists, the hated "oppressor class" is men, for homosexuals, it is heterosexuals, for trans-sexuals, it is cis-sexuals, for non-whites, it is whites.[91] Rejecting the Christian notion that "all have sinned and fallen short of the glory of God" (Romans 3:23), virtue is inherent in the "oppressed" and vice is inherent in the "oppressor."[92]

US Air Force Chief of Staff General Charles Q. Brown provides a poignant example of critical race theory thinking in action. When he was serving as commander for the Pacific Air Force (PACAF), and while wearing civilian clothes, Brown parked outside a military store in his designated parking spot. Not recognizing Brown in his civilian clothes, someone said "that is the PACAF parking spot." Brown replied, "Yes, I am the PACAF."[93] General Brown, who is black, could have assumed that the speaker

---

[91] One would think that the "oppressor" class would vary by population, location, and time. For example, there are more Han Chinese men in China and Indian men in India than white men in the USA and Europe combined. For millennia, oppression in China and India has at least equaled that of anywhere else in the world.

[92] It is hard to escape being amused by critical theory advocates who argue, with bright red faces and clenched fists, that certain groups are oppressive, while denying the objective reality of groups at all. How can heterosexuals oppress homosexuals if sex is a continuum, not binary? How can people with fairer skin discriminate against people with darker skin if race does not exist?

[93] The Story Behind the Air Force Chief of Staff's 'Kicking Butt' Recruiting Ad, https://www.military.com/daily-news/2021/08/07/story-behind-air-force-chief-of-staffs-kicking-butt-recruiting-ad.html.

was just trying to prevent him, an unrecognized man, from being ticketed by the base police. Instead, Brown uses the story to rage against what he deems is institutional racism in the Air Force.

Brown could have assumed the best and been charitable towards the person, who was undoubtedly mortified by his clumsiness. Instead, Brown chose to interpret the interaction in the most divisive, angriest, and least forgiving way possible. Even if the comment was meant as a racial slur, and General Brown can never know, he could have chosen to forgive. Jesus taught "but if you do not forgive others their sins, your Father will not forgive yours (Matthew 6:15)." We must all beware.

In "critical theories" such as queer, feminist, and race, good and evil return with a vengeance. "Good" is anything which builds up the oppressed and tears down the oppressor. "Evil" is anything which does the opposite, or which to a "good" person appears to do the opposite. The more "oppressed" groups a person belongs to, the more virtuous they are. So, a black, Buddhist, transgender man (biologically a woman) is "better" than a Hispanic Muslim heterosexual woman. A heterosexual, Christian, white male is the worst of all.

Morality is reduced to considerations of one's group and its power status. No amount of virtue is necessary to justify the oppressed, for they are justified by being oppressed. No amount of repentance is sufficient to sanctify the oppressor because they are condemned by being oppressors. Individuals in oppressed groups share in the righteousness of their oppressed predecessors, and individuals in oppressor groups are forever stained by and responsible for the sins of their oppressive ancestors, no matter how long ago these sins occurred.

Unlike the Biblical teaching that each person is responsible for what he or she does (Deuteronomy 24:16, Ezekiel 18:19-20, Galatians 6:4-8), such critical philosophies hold that "oppressors" are responsible for their own misdoings, their contemporaries' misdoings, their ancestors' misdoings, and for the misdoings of the oppressed classes. The oppressed are responsible for nothing since they lack power. As in Marxism, utopia arrives when the oppressor class is defeated and destroyed and the formerly oppressed usher in an "enlightened" future.[94]

Jesus told His disciples to forgive "seventy times seven," (Matthew 18:21-22) but Christian forgiveness is foreign, and even unwanted, in secular humanism, Marxism, and its related "critical" belief systems. The Christian hope of achieving "as good as possible" justice now and ultimate justice in the world to come is condemned by those who reject the notion of life after death.[95] The religious fervor of "wokeism," an awkward combination of these secular beliefs with the quasi-Buddhist belief that only its adherents are "awake," arises because wokist acolytes fix their hopes on political and governmental action in this short life.

People who believe in secular humanism, Marxism, and the critical theories will live less than eighty years, on average. They will often not marry, have no children, and fix their hopes for meaning on what they can accomplish through politics during their lifetime. Such is a heavy burden to bear.

Time and space prevent discussion of the basics of all major religions and philosophies. We have identified some key differences in these faiths. In later chapters, we will readily see how those differences impact the ways that adherents to each religion or philosophy try to influence those around them. We can now investigate how members of these religions and adherents to these philosophies use the arts to shape their world.

---

[94] Like everything else, individuals vary in their understanding of any philosophy. What is described here is the philosophical construct of these positions.
[95] Remember, after all, that it was the Christians who led the fight against slavery in the West, and West ended slavery long before most other cultures.

Discussion Questions for lessons, book, and Bible studies

1. Describe Islam
2. Describe Hinduism
3. Describe Buddhism
4. Describe one other non-Christian faith
5. Describe Secular Humanism
6. Describe Marxism
7. Describe modern critical philosophies, such as post-colonial, feminist, queer, disability, fat, and critical race theory.
8. What is an appropriate Christian response to each of these belief systems?
9. What does the Bible say about the beliefs and actions noted in this chapter?

4

HOW DO MUSLIMS USE THE ARTS TO SHAPE THE WORLD?

Leafing through the book *Islamic Art and Architecture* by Robert Hillenbrand, several observations come to mind. Architecture, textiles, furnishings, and calligraphy predominate. From the Dome of the Rock (Jerusalem, 691), the first major surviving monument of the Umayyad dynasty (661-750), to the Selimiye Mosque (Edirne, Turkey, 1575), the masterpiece of Mimar Sinan and one of the greatest achievements of Islamic architecture, Muslims were famous for building. In addition to mosques, architects designed and built notable mausoleums, such as the Taj Mahal (Agra, India, 1632), and palaces, such as the Topkapi Palace (Istanbul, 1478).

Following the example of the trader and later Prophet Mohammad, Muslims constructed caravansaries a day's journey apart on major trade routes throughout their domains. Though commonplace structures, these caravansaries boasted architectural flourishes as exemplified by the arches and wall decorations of the Rabat-I Malik (1078) in Uzbekistan.[96] The man-made slave harbor at Alanya (Turkey, 1228) provided safe and secret galleries for ship building but was also a fine example of architecture and

---

[96] Robert Hillenbrand, *Islamic Art and Architecture*, World of Art (New York: Thames and Hudson, 1999), 109.

Muslims and Art

engineering.[97] In fact, the thirteenth century Seljuks of Rum had an unrivaled building tradition in the Islamic world.[98]

The emphasis on architecture was the natural response to the Middle Eastern environment. Solomon, Nebuchadnezzar, and Herod the Great were earlier kings in the Fertile Crescent who were noted for their construction projects. These included the Temple in Jerusalem, the Hanging Gardens of Babylon, and the Herodium in Palestine. Islam arose from the Middle East, and so structures built by Muslims were often built of stone, which was plentiful. Many of these buildings endure today and speak volumes about the Islamic architectural tradition. By contrast, early Northern European structures such as stave churches were constructed of wood, which was plentiful locally, but degraded with time and humidity. Few of these churches survive, and so speak less about the earliest architectural traditions in the north.

Textiles were another critical means of Islamic artistic expression. One of the Caliph's palaces boasted 38,000 wall hangings, as reported by awed Byzantine ambassadors.[99] Textiles are the natural accompaniment of architecture, especially in hot, dry, climates where stone is the primary building material. Textiles can dampen sound, subdivide rooms, provide privacy, and transform the character of spaces. For example, hanging rugs with winter colors can be replaced with those of summer colors in the appropriate season. Textiles are portable, valuable, and can be readily bought and sold, thus providing a store of wealth and a source of valuable liquidity in premodern financial markets.[100] The Islamic tradition of art in tapestries continues today. Created by craftsmen, typically in government-sponsored factories, such

---

[97] Hillenbrand, 120.
[98] Hillenbrand, 121.
[99] Hillenbrand, 49.
[100] Hillenbrand, 50.

handmade tapestries can be magnificent, showing flowers and other natural or stylized designs in vibrant colors.

Furnishings for buildings, another essential complement to architecture, could be ornate. Bronze or ceramic jugs, tableware, and even glasses portrayed flowers or scenes from day-to-day life. A Fatimid lustre bowl (11th-12th century) shows cock fighting, while another displays a mounted falconer.[101] Items were frequently gilded or inlaid with silver or gold in wealthy households. The Baptistère de Saint Louis (c 1300) is a large bronze, gold and silver bowl made by Mohammad ibn al-Zain. It was captured in war (or given to French royalty) and was used to baptize infants of the French royal family until 1856.[102]

Early in the history of Islam, the Umayyad rulers employed Byzantine artists to adorn their palaces and mosques with realistic pictures of plants and animals.[103] With the codification of Islamic law, however, concerns about idolatry grew. Calligraphy became the preferred visual art in the Sunni tradition.

There are four traditional schools of Islamic jurisprudence: *Shafiyya*, *Hanafi*, *Maliki*, and *Hanbali*. Naqib al-Misri's (d 769) *Reliance of the Traveler* is a *Shafiyya* compilation of sacred Islamic law and overlaps more than 75% between the schools.[104] It includes pertinent notes from each school to provide the reader with a trustworthy summary. *Reliance of the Traveler* states that makers of pictures will go to the fire.[105] Such laws, predictably,

---

[101] Hillenbrand, 80-81.
[102] Hillenbrand, 154.
[103] Malise Ruthven, *Islam in the world*, 3rd ed. (Oxford: Oxford University Press, 2006), 193.
[104] Aḥmad ibn Lu'lu' Ibn al-Naqīb, Reliance of the Traveller: The Classic Manual of Islamic Sacred Law 'umdat Al-Salik, rev. ed., trans. Nuh Ha Mim Keller (Beltsville, MD, U.S.A.: Amana Publications, 2011), p vii.
[105] Aḥmad ibn Lu'lu' Ibn al-Naqīb, *Reliance of the Traveller: The Classic Manual of Islamic Sacred Law 'umdat Al-Salik*, rev. ed., trans. Nu Ha Mim Keller (Beltsville, MD, U.S.A.: Amana Publications, 2011), p44.0, expanded in w50.0.

had a chilling effect on Muslims' interest in painting. Muslims generally do not illustrate the *Quran* for fear of idolatry. Instead, they write Quranic verses in magnificent calligraphy on their buildings, tapestries, furnishings, and other items. When the Ottomans conquered Constantinople in 1453, Sultan Mehmed II (1432-1481) changed the legendary church, the *Hagia Sophia*, into a mosque by removing Christian relics, plastering over Christian mosaics, adding minarets, and writing Quranic verses in calligraphy on many of the newly bare places.[106] The Tomb of Tamerlane (1336-1405) in Samarkand uses Islamic calligraphy in its décor.[107] The *Shahada*, "there is no God but Allah, and Mohammad is His prophet," is frequently used as architectural calligraphy, as well as on flags. To some, Islamic calligraphy is a form of "visual music."[108]

Book painting has a long history in the Islamic World, but copies of the *Quran* are often adorned with designs and symbols rather than pictures. Unlike artists in the West, there is little evidence of a significant naturalistic painting tradition among Muslims. Muslim artists have historically had an uneasy relationship with sculpture. The bronze Griffin of Pisa was probably made in Moorish Spain but consciously avoids looking natural.[109]

---

[106] The Hagia Sophia was built by Byzantine emperor Justinian I in AD 360. It remained a church until the Ottoman Turks conquered Constantinople in 1453. The Hagia Sophia was turned into a mosque, then a secular museum by Ataturk in 1934, and back into a mosque by Recep Erdogan in 2020.
[107] Hillenbrand, 214.
[108] Hillenbrand, 67.
[109] Hillenbrand, 180.

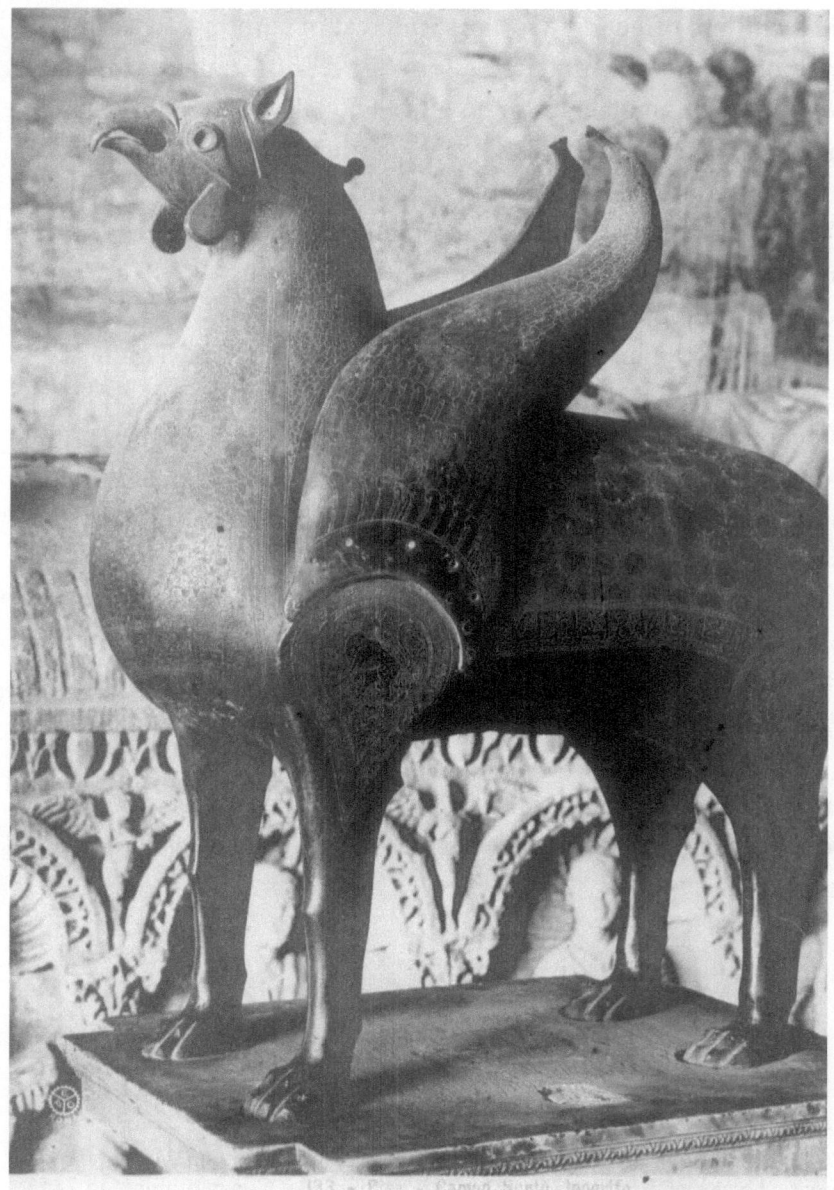

Pisa Griffin in the Camposanto in Pisa c. 1890-1900[110]

---

[110] Gustave Chauffourier, *Photo of Pisa Griffin in the Camposanto in Pisa*, 1900, Online Image, *Wikipedia*, 1900, https://en.wikipedia.org/wiki/Pisa_Griffin#/media/File:Hippogriff1.jpg.

The Islamic world, especially Persia, has a rich tradition of poetry. *The Rubiyat of Omar Khayyam* (1048-1131) is one of the most famous collections of Persian poems. *One Thousand and One Nights* is a renowned compilation of Middle Eastern and South Asian adventure stories from the 8th to the 13th centuries. Islam does not forbid poetry.

Food arts are important in Islam due to Quranic dietary restrictions. For example, Muslims are not permitted eat pork (Quran 2:173) or drink alcohol (Quran 2:219). Food approved in the Quran are dates (19:25), grain (Quran 78:14), ginger (Quran 76:17), grain, vines, herbs, olives, sheep (Quran 80:27-29), figs (Quran 95:1), honey (Quran 16:69-70), milk (Quran 47:15), fish (Quran 18:61), pomegranates (Quran 55:68), grapes (Quran 16:11), plantains (Quran 56:29), gourds (Quran 37:146), mint (Quran 55:12), beef (Quran 2:67), rams (Quran 37:107), goats (Quran 6:143), quail (Quran 20:80), and other fowl (Quran 56:21). Many other foods are permissible.

Islamic law discourages the use of music. *Reliance of the Traveler* forbids "musical instruments, flutes, strings, crucifixes, and the affair of the pre-Islamic period of ignorance."[111] It later reads "Allah will pour molten lead into the ears of whoever sits listening to a songstress."[112] Subsequent passages forbid mandolin, lute, cymbals, and flute but allow the tambourine. Singing is offensive except for specific circumstances including singing the Sunna, the teachings, deeds, and sayings of Mohammad, and singing at weddings. Islamic law expressly permits dancing.[113]

In practice, music is a part of Islamic traditions, especially among minority groups and in the Western world. Sufis sometimes

---

[111] Aḥmad ibn Lu'lu' Ibn al-Naqīb, r40.1 (1), 774.
[112] Aḥmad ibn Lu'lu' Ibn al-Naqīb, r40.1 (2), 775.
[113] Aḥmad ibn Lu'lu' Ibn al-Naqīb, r40.4. 776.

Religion and Art

use reed flutes in their *dhikrs* (devotional acts).[114] The Ahmadiyya movement among African Americans in the mid-twentieth century merged black jazz traditions with Islamic worship.[115] American Druze may use music in their religious services.[116] The *Nizari* Ismailis are another Muslim minority group in the United States that uses music.

Dance is especially important in the Sufi tradition of the *Mawlawiya* (Whirling Dervishes). Dating from the 12th century, the circular motion of the dance connotes the movement of the dancer's spirit around other living things.[117] Participants accelerate and decelerate their movements and attain a disciplined ecstasy, which onlookers feel as well. This dance was traditionally not self-conscious or theatrical, as is ballet, tap, jazz, modern, and other styles. Rather it was self-abandoning, as the dancer sought *Allah*. This has changed as troupes of dervishes dance for audiences around the world.

Ceremonies marking important life events use the arts to teach, to encourage, and to inspire the bride, groom, and onlookers in their lives and their religion. Marriage and childbearing are considered religious duties in Islam and so weddings are sometimes performed in mosques.[118] In a traditional wedding ceremony in Morocco, a woman called a *nakasha* paints a henna design on the hands and feet of the bride. The bride wears a *negafa*, a long and brightly colored silk undergarment with a transparent overgarment.[119]

---

[114] Marshall G S. Hodgson, *The Venture of Islam: Conscience and History in a World Civilization* (Chicago: University of Chicago Press, 1974), 250.
[115] Yvonne Yazbeck Haddad and Jane I. Smith, eds., *The Oxford Handbook of American Islam*, Oxford Handbooks (New York: Oxford University Press, 2014), 147.
[116] Haddad, 143.
[117] Ruthven, 255.
[118] Carolyn Mordecai, *Weddings, Dating, and Love Customs of Cultures Worldwide* (Phoenix AZ: Nittany Publishers, 1999). 22-24
[119] Mordecai, 56-57.

Muslims and Art

After a normal death, a Muslim who dies has his body washed and prepared carefully for burial. A family member of the deceased leads a funeral prayer.[120] However, if a Muslim dies in a *jihad* (holy war), attendants remove the war gear but neither remove the bloodstained clothes nor wash or otherwise prepare the corpse. No funeral prayer is spoken. The "martyr" is buried as he died. Islamic burial traditions are vastly different for a man going to judgment (a normal death) than for a martyr going to Paradise (a soldier killed in a *jihad*). Insofar as these traditions represent a type of "art," Islam uses these traditions to honor those killed in *jihad*, thereby encouraging others to fight in *jihad*.

How have Muslims used these arts to shape the world to promote their world view? The political, temporal, and earthly focus of Islam is reflected in Islamic art. The governor of Kufa, Ibn b. Musa built a fortified residence for himself outside modern Ukhaidir, Iraq.[121] His palace mixed security and ceremony, a recurrent theme in Islamic architecture. Such buildings served to highlight the grandeur of the occupant while ensuring that enemies think twice before challenging them. Leaders of the first Muslim empire, the Umayyads (661-750), used art to express and enhance their military and material glory.[122] The Saffavids of Persia (1501-1736) reflected security and ceremony in their capital city of Isfahan as well.

Muslims used art, as all other peoples did, to praise their great people and add legitimacy to the ruling dynasty. A Turkish stucco relief from Rayy, Anatolia (late 12th century) honors Seljuk Sultan Tughril II (d 1194). Items made in Spain had Arabic calligraphic messages like "Glory to our Lord, the Sultan."[123]

---

[120] al-Misri, 235-236.
[121] Hillenbrand, 41.
[122] Hillenbrand, 16.
[123] Hillenbrand, 191.

Religion and Art

Ornamented writing also helped Muslims learn about and remember the *Quran*.

In accordance with their scriptures, Muslims are limited in the types of art they can consume or produce. Nonetheless, Islamic art has long been used to influence people to become Muslims. Failing that, it encourages outsiders to adopt, or at least tolerate, an Islamic world view and Islamic practices. Islamic art has been employed to support the reigns of caliphs and sultans. Such art effectively glorifies Muslim rulers and terrifies, or at least warns, those who would oppose them. Finally, Islamic art has been used to enhance the lives of individual Muslims.

Discussion Questions for lessons, book, and Bible study

1. Describe key arts that Muslims have used to shape their world.
2. Describe some of the Islamic prohibitions on art.
3. Describe some Islamic wedding and funeral customs.
4. Describe one way that you have seen Muslims using the arts to shape the world in your life.
5. How do Muslim artistic practices show themselves in jihad in the modern day?
6. Share some thoughts about sharing the gospel with Muslims.
7. What does the Bible say about the beliefs and actions noted in this chapter?

5

How do Hindus use the arts to shape the world?

On Memorial Day 2016, I visited the Hindu Durga Temple in Fairfax Station, Virginia. The main portion of the temple was a large, high-ceilinged room with a small, low stage on one side. Small shrines to Hindu deities were inset in the inside walls, and larger covered structures (Greek - *aediculae*) housed major Hindu deities in the middle. Worshippers entered the room without shoes. They prayed, left money, and performed rituals at the idol of each god or goddess, moving clockwise between shrines, and skipping whichever deities they did not wish to worship. One ritual involved pouring milk and later water over a large, smooth rock, shaped like a large egg or a short, fat phallus. A priest led the people in singing and chanting (*kirtan*), accompanied by drums but no other instruments. After finishing the rituals, the priest gave each worshipper a carnation, an almond, and a banana, symbolizing the blessing of the gods, or god, upon them.

The idols were well made, with colorful clothing. The temple was light. Artificial flowers, hand bells, cups and plates abounded. Most idols had fair skin and portrayed the right hand with palm forward and fingers pointing up; a hand position signifying that the god was blessing the worshipper. Hanuman, the Monkey god, and Ganesh, the Elephant god, were featured. The black skinned goddess Kali, with her necklace of skulls, her many arms holding weapons and one grasping the severed head of an enemy, had a shrine. The exterior featured off-white, gently curved towers such as are common in northern, Aryan, India, and a six-level pyramid frequently seen in the Dravidian south. The entire process took Hindu worshippers twenty to thirty minutes, but the variation was great. The Hindu priest took pains to ensure that the idols were well cared for.

Consistent with *darsan* (seeing or being seen by the divine) as noted earlier, Hinduism knows no limitation to artistic expression. According to the *Vishnudharmottara Purana* (part 3, chapter 43),

> A proper painting brings on prosperity, removes adversity, cleanses and curbs anxiety, augments future good, causes unequalled and pure delight, kills evils of bad dreams, and pleases the household deity – rules of painting should also be applied to carvings in iron, stone, wood, or clay modeling.[124]

Hindus have a high regard for painting and sculpture and use them to decorate objects, homes, temples, palaces, and other buildings. Subjects include daily life, kings, erotica, and the lives of Hindu gods. The popular *Gita Govinda*, the love story of Krishna and Radha, composed by the 12th century poet Jayadeva, was prolifically illustrated. Hindus believed the erotic sculptures at the Visvanatha and Lakshmana temples in Khajuraho (11 century) had a magico-protective effect, as intercourse had generative powers.[125]

According to many Hindus with whom I have spoken, Hindus today do not believe that an idol is a god. Rather they believe that each god indwells his or her idol, meets with each worshipper, and blesses him or her. Craftsmen produce the best

---

[124] Heather Elgood, *Hinduism and the Religious Arts*, Religion and the Arts (London: Cassell, 2000), 89.
[125] Elgood, 107.

idols possible, for no god would want to dwell in an ugly idol. Idols are created in specific ways and with a specific look – there is no room for artistic license. Priests feed, clothe, and otherwise maintain the idol. Worshippers enter, and each gives gifts and pays homage (*bhakti*) to the god in the idol. For their part, the deity reciprocates with a blessing (*prasada*), and the transaction is complete. The worshipper leaves with his or her desired blessing.[126]

The temple, with its architecture and furnishings, is the most characteristic artistic expression of Hinduism.[127] The core function of a Hindu temple is to protect the shrine of the deity whose idol is contained therein, to be the sacred space where gods live and man visits, and ultimately to link the gods and man.[128] In Hindu thought, man is trapped in the never-ending cycle of life, death, and rebirth (*samsara*). For Buddhists and some Buddhist influenced Hindus, *samsara* is really an illusion (*maya*). Man strives to escape the cycle (*moksha*) and merge with the universal spirit (*Brahman*). The gods need to be roused and cajoled to help humans achieve their goals, whether temporal (such as making money) or eternal (achieving *moksha*).

Hindu gods prefer to reside in natural features such as mountains, rivers, trees, and caves, so Hindu temples are built to be like these natural homes. Hindu Temples are symbolic representations of the universe and are meant to be in geometrical harmony with the cosmos (*Vimana*). If Hindu temples do not meet these standards, the poor architecture will discourage gods from visiting the temple, thus impairing worshippers' ability to commune with the gods, receive the temporal blessing, and ultimately achieve *moksha*.

---

[126] Elgood, 91.
[127] George Mitchell, *The Hindu Temple* (Chicago: University of Chicago Press, 1988), 14.
[128] Mitchell, 60.

Temples generally have a horizontal axis running east-west and a vertical axis ascending to a high point suggesting a mountain peak. Just as temple exteriors evoke thoughts of mountains, interiors often resemble caves.[129] In some cases, the small, intimate interiors speak of the inside of the womb from which all men are birthed. The center of a temple is a sacred square of nine smaller squares or other geometric design (*mandala*) representing the universe and the universal spirit (*Brahman*). Surrounding squares represent the sun, the moon, other astronomical bodies, and other Hindu deities. The central area can also represent the cosmic man. The Durga Temple was an exception; it had a spacious interior without a noticeable mandala.

Northern India has the highest mountain ranges in the world and the northern temple style (*nagara*) includes a mountain peak (*sikhara*) and a tiered layer (*bhumi*).[130] Southern India is flatter, though it still has mountains, and the southern temple style has four elements: a pyramidal temple (*Vimana*), porches (*mandapas*), gate pyramids (*gopurams*), and pillared hallways. If the northern architecture resembles mountains, the southern reflects palaces. Both styles impress worshippers with power and transcendence, encouraging people to feel the presence of the gods they believe are within. The Hindu Temple of Washington DC is an American example of the attempt to make the people feel the gods, and of Hindus using attractive architecture to shape their world.

In Hinduism, the icons within the temple are as important as the temple itself. Outside reliefs of gods, battles, and myths are common and door guardians (*dvarapalas*) often protect the entrance, as angels or other door guardians may serve the same artistic function in cathedrals. I did not see either in the Durga Temple.

---

[129] Mitchell, 69.
[130] Mitchell, 69.

Religion and Art

Writing arts such as prose and poetry figure prominently in Hinduism. The *Mahabharata* and the *Ramayana* are two famous epic poems of Hindu scripture (*smrti*). The former contains the *Bhagavata Gita*, one of the most beloved *puranas* in Hindu scripture. The latter was made into a television series in 1986, the *Ramayan*, which became the most watched series ever.[131] It was remade and rebroadcast in 2008.

Forty percent of Hindus espouse a vegetarian diet and 80% limit meat.[132] Killing animals and consuming meat is discouraged (Yajur Veda 12:32). Milk, eggs, and other foods requiring refrigeration should be avoided. Hindu chefs have a variety of ways to make vegetables look and taste good.[133]

Hindu music includes the *bhajan*, a Hindu devotional song, and the *kirtan*, the communal call-and-response chanting of mantras, which includes instruments and dance.[134] *Bhakti* traditions emphasize the importance of *bhajan* in achieving *moksha*, while *kirtan* practices are rooted in the *Vedas*.

Traditional Hindu weddings are replete with art and meaning. The bride applies sandalwood paste to her groom's forehead.[135] The groom places a red dot on his bride's forehead to signify that she is married. The couple tosses small amounts of puffed rice and purified butter into a fire, which represents a deity.[136] They then circumambulate the fire in the *sapta-padi*,

---

[131] Reigning Hindu TV Gods of India Have Viewers Glued to Their Sets, http://www.wsj.com/articles/SB893132809466500000.
[132] Manolo Corichi, "Eight-In-Ten Indians Limit Meat in Their Diets, and Four-In-Ten Consider Themselves Vegetarian," Pew Research Center, July 8, 2021, https://www.pewresearch.org/short-reads/2021/07/08/eight-in-ten-indians-limit-meat-in-their-diets-and-four-in-ten-consider-themselves-vegetarian/.
[133] Sebastian Pole, *Ayurvedic Medicine: The Principles of Traditional Practice* (London; Philadelphia: Singing Dragon, Cop, 2013). 104.
[134] H Wayne House, *Charts of World Religions*, Zondervancharts (Grand Rapids, Mich.: Zondervan, 2006), 85.
[135] Mordecai, 21.
[136] Agni is the traditional Hindu fire god.

signifying what they will do in their common journey through life:[137]

1. Earning a living
2. Living a healthy lifestyle
3. Showing concern for each other's welfare
4. Enhancing each other's pleasure.
5. Spending time together
6. Desiring (and having) children
7. Adapting to the other person

The parents of the bride give presents to the groom and tie cotton around the couple, signifying unity and blessings. Finally, the couple places floral love necklaces on each other, and the priest chants mantras. The artistry behind the ceremony seals the messages, duties, and commitments inherent in Hindu life.

Hindu *bhakti* attempts to communicate love and devotion from a worshipper to his or her god. In some traditions, *bhakti* is portrayed as erotic love between man, usually playing the role of a god, and a woman, typically playing the role of a worshipper.[138] The courtesan appeared often in such literature, engaged in erotic song and dance. As the culture changed and courtesans diminished in importance, song and dance traditions faded as well.[139] Many were reinterpreted and reclaimed as *bhakti*. The Islamic *Sufi* tradition and the Christian traditions of Hildegard of Bingen also incorporate images of human romance and divine love.

Hindus do not historically consider themselves part of a missionary faith, but nonetheless use the arts to educate others about their faith and influence others towards their world view.

---

[137] Mordecai, 21.
[138] Attipat Krishnaswami Ramanujan, David Dean Shulman, and Velcheru Narayana Rao, *When God Is a Customer: Telugu Courtesan Songs by Ksetrayya and Others* (Delhi: Oxford University Press, 1995), 2.
[139] Ramanujan, Shulman, and Rao, 26-28.

Religion and Art

The beauty and diversity of Hindu art lends a strong appeal to that faith in the minds of some. Hinduism is growing in America, largely through immigration, and Hindus are expected to continue to comprise about 15% of the world's population through 2050.[140]

---

[140] Pew Research Center, Hindus, http://www.pewforum.org/2015/04/02/hindus/, accessed 15 Aug 2016.

Discussion Questions for lessons, book, and Bible studies

1. Describe key arts that Hindus have used to shape their world.
2. Describe some of the Hindu practices in art.
3. Describe some Hindu wedding customs.
4. Describe one way that you have seen Hindus using the arts to shape the world in your life.
5. Share some thoughts about sharing the gospel with Hindus.
6. What does the Bible say about the beliefs and actions noted in this chapter?

6

HOW DO BUDDHISTS USE THE ARTS TO SHAPE THE WORLD?

Siddhartha Gautama, The Buddha, had a mixed view of the arts. His path to enlightenment involved renouncing desires and eliminating illusion (*maya*), while many of the arts provoked desire and fostered illusion. He considered singing to be like wailing, dancing to be madness, and laughter to be childish.[141] The Buddha also objected to theater. At the same time, the *Lotus Sutra*, an important scripture in Mahayana Buddhism, tells adherents to build mausoleums ("stupas") for the Enlightened Ones, the Buddhas.[142] The *Lotus Sutra* also encourages making or adorning sculptures and painting images of Buddhas.[143] Buddhists applaud such works of art even if young children at play make them.

Buddhist monasteries began as temporary structures built in the monsoon season that were tall enough for the monks to crouch inside. Long, flexible (often bamboo) poles formed the frame, and grass, leaves, and mats covered the structure. The entryway was peaked. Later, rock caves were carved with this ribbed style and

---

[141] Bhikkhu Bodhi, *The Numerical Discourses of the Buddha: A Translation of the Anguttara Nikaya*, Book of Threes (Boston: Wisdom Publications, 2012), 107(5), 342

[142] Gene Reeves, trans., *The Lotus Sutra: A Contemporary Translation of a Buddhist Classic* (Somerville, MA: Wisdom Publications, 2008), 92.

[143] Reeves, 93.

eventually buildings adopted the same architecture. The cave at Bhaja, west of Poona, is a notable example.[144]

Stupas form the central monument of Buddhist monasteries. They are often covered with relief sculptures describing the historical life of Buddha. The 44-meter-high, 27-meter diameter, *Dhamekh Stupa* in Sarnath, the place where the Buddha taught his first disciples, is a striking representation. It is built of brick on a stone brace and boasts ornamental stonework and artistic design.[145]

Painting and calligraphy have been prominent in Buddhist art. Human images of the Buddha became more common in the first century AD and demonstrated Roman influences. The Buddha was portrayed with features like the god Apollo and clothing similar to a toga. Images of the Buddha developed their modern form in the Golden Age of India under the Gupta Empire (4th-6th centuries). Literature is important to Buddhists. Monks are not permitted to discuss their own enlightenment for fear of pride, but they can write of their spiritual liberation in poetry. From the days of the Buddha, 264 poems penned by monks and 73 by nuns survive today.[146]

---

[144] Schumann, 175.
[145] Schumann, 67.
[146] Schumann, 180.

Religion and Art

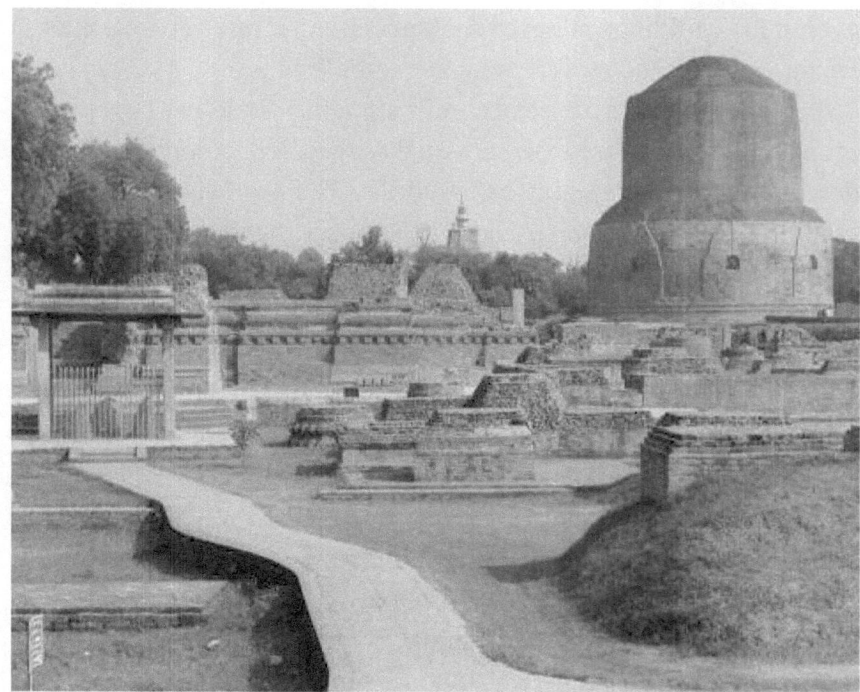

Dhamekh Stupa Sarnath, Varanasi, Uttar Pradesh 221007, India.[147]

    Despite the views of the Buddha as noted in Theravada scripture, many strains of Buddhism not only encourage producing but also consuming art. Buddhists visit stupas to make offerings, adorn the images, perform with instruments, sing, prostrate themselves, or exclaim "Hail to the Buddha." In so doing they "fulfill the Buddha Way."[148] Such acts confer lasting merit upon the actor and inch him or her ever more closely to the pathway of enlightenment and ultimate deliverance (*moksha*) from the cycle of life (*samsara*).

---

[147] Ekabhishek, *Monastery around Dhamek Stupa, Sarnath*, November 12, 2010, Online Image, *Wikimedia Commons*, November 12, 2010, https://commons.wikimedia.org/wiki/File:Monastery_around_Dhamek_stupa_Sarnath.jpg.

[148] Reeves, 94-95.

Images serve to remind Buddhists of the spiritual qualities of holy beings, such as *Arahants*, *Bodhisatvas*, or *Buddhas*. In many traditions, believers see images as being infused with the spirit and power of the personality portrayed. These works of art are considered so powerful, especially the eyes, that workers cover the idol's face to prevent being harmed by the spirit in the image. Artists will only paint the eyes of the idol while looking into a mirror, or a polished shield, as the legendary Perseus did when he slayed the Medusa. In Theraveda Buddhism, a monk places a relic or scriptures into the newly created idol, then chants over it for several hours, to consecrate it.[149]

The *Komuso* monks of Zen Buddhism were famous for their *Honkyoku* music, traditionally played on bamboo flutes.[150] The use of drums in playing complex rhythms to accompany ritualized chanting is another important part of Buddhist life. The *Damaru* is a small drum, and the *Ghanta* is a bell used in Vajrayana Buddhist rituals.[151]

Rhythmic chanting is a key activity in the *Sangha*, the assembly of Buddhist monks. Chants may be done to gain a good harvest, ward off animal, human, or ghostly enemies, cure illness, increase wealth, please the gods, or increase karmic fruitfulness.[152] However effective one may believe these chants to be, rhythmic chanting, especially when the words are pleasant, can be soothing for both chanters and listeners.

In 8th century Japan, Buddhist emperor Shomu introduced six schools of Chinese Buddhism.[153] In his capital of Nara, Shomu built the primary monastery of the *Kegon* school with an 18-meter-tall statue of Vairocana Buddha. The image represented the central

---

[149] Harvey, 248.
[150] Ronald Nelson, "The International Shakuhachi Society," www.komuso.com, accessed June 17, 2017, http://www.komuso.com/top/index.pl.
[151] House, chart 71.
[152] Harvey, 249.
[153] Harvey, 226.

point of spiritual and temporal power in the realm. Uplifting Buddhist art proliferated. In his move, Shomu opened up a country wide road system, to allow people to travel between cities and temples. He also improved writing, as literate monks taught illiterate peasants. For Shomu, the outcome was to concentrate power in his hands.[154]

As with other religions, Buddhists use the arts to understand and express themselves and to influence others. Buddhist architecture reflects the earliest days of the faith, and images, whether paintings or statuary, show the appeal of the founder. Verse allows individual Buddhists to shout their thoughts, words, actions, and emotions, to themselves and to the world.

There are many parallels between the art of the non-Christian religions and that of Jews and Christians. Compare, for example, the following passage written by Vimala, who was a prostitute before she became a Buddhist nun,[155] with the warning of the harlot in Proverbs 7.

Vimala, Buddhist nun

Conceited was I once of my complexion
My figure, beauty, popularity
I trusted that my youth would never dwindle
In short: I was unknowing and naïve.
Having adorned with jewelry this body
And with make-up, enticing for young men,
I waited at the brothel door, desirous
For victims, like a hunter setting snares.
I showed myself when I put on my jewels
And shamelessly revealed my hidden charms,
In practicing diverse tricks of seduction
I had my fun with a great many men.
Today I am bald shaven, clad as a nun…

---

[154] Harvey, 226.
[155] Schumann, 183.

Proverbs 7:6-23

For at the window of my house
I looked out through my lattice,
And I saw among the naive,
And discerned among the youths
A young man lacking sense,
Passing through the street near her corner;
And he takes the way to her house,
In the twilight, in the evening,
In the middle of the night and in the darkness.
And behold, a woman comes to meet him,
Dressed as a harlot and cunning of heart.
She is boisterous and rebellious,
Her feet do not remain at home;
She is now in the streets, now in the squares,
And lurks by every corner.
So she seizes him and kisses him
And with a brazen face she says to him:
I was due to offer peace offerings;
Today I have paid my vows.
Therefore, I have come out to meet you,
To seek your presence earnestly, and I have found you.
I have spread my couch with coverings,
With colored linens of Egypt.
I have sprinkled my bed
With myrrh, aloes and cinnamon.
Come, let us drink our fill of love until morning;
Let us delight ourselves with caresses.
For my husband is not at home,
He has gone on a long journey;
He has taken a bag of money with him,
At the full moon he will come home."
With her many persuasions she entices him;
With her flattering lips she seduces him.
Suddenly he follows her
As an ox goes to the slaughter,
Or as one in fetters to the discipline of a fool,
Until an arrow pierces through his liver;
As a bird hastens to the snare,
So he does not know that it will cost him his life.

Verses like this reveal the universal human condition and how different religions try to address it. Vimala's portion is a self-portrait and consistent with the strong individualistic focus of Buddhism. After all, each adherent must work out his or her own enlightenment, albeit sometimes in community and always with similar methods. The Proverbs account is a story that a narrator tells of other people, emphasizing the community focus of the ancient Hebrews. Parallels such as these between non-Christian holy books and the Bible can help all parties understand each other better. They can also be useful in teaching and demonstrating the grace of Christ.

A Buddhist diet will emphasize vegetarianism, abstention from alcohol, and frequent fasting. Milk and dairy products which do not involve killing are tolerated. As with the Hindu diet, there are many ways to employ the culinary arts to make a vegetarian diet appealing and delicious.

Buddhist weddings will sometimes boast a tea ceremony where the groom, bride, and a host prepare a week prior to the wedding. The *bhikkhu* burns floral incense to begin the ceremony.[156] The couple and attendees chant the Heart of Wisdom Sutra. The officiator prompts a public confession and then forgiveness. The *bhikkhu* places a fresh leaf into water and places three drops of the water on to the forehead of bride and groom. He wipes them off with a dull knife, thus symbolizing cleanliness. Incense is burned, and then the couple recite their vows while holding a strand of *Ojuzu* or *Mala* beads. Man and wife exchange rings, and the *bhikkhu* concludes the ceremony. Each element functions artistically to bless the couple and others around with the duty, and beauty, of what the couple has begun.

Buddhist funeral rites begin when the family notifies the *bhikkhu (bonze)* of the passing. Rice, gold, or coins may be placed

---

[156] Mordecai, 5.

Buddhists and Art

inside the mouth of the deceased.[157] Family members wear white clothes as they prepare the body for burial. The *bonze*, a Buddhist monk who officiates the ceremony, begins the *Service of Encasketing*. Two altars are present, the Deceased Altar and the Buddha Altar.[158] The Deceased Altar contains incense, flowers, fruits, and food (a boiled egg atop rice). The Buddha Altar, placed at right angles to the Deceased Altar, has incense, candles, and fruits. The *Bonze* then strikes wooden bells and prays. At the graveside, the *Bonze* prays and gives a final benediction, including holy water and incense.[159] Buddhists recommend cremation. Post burial services will continue for seven weeks, the idea being that repeated services aid in transmigration to a different body and a new life.

As with the other faiths noted above, these Buddhist life transition ceremonies, both in their art and ritual, play a huge role in the lives of the attendees. Those involved shape the world as they understand it and encourage others to do likewise.

---

[157] Ed Staufer, Jimmie R Duncan, and William Lotz, *Fire Chaplain Training Manual* (Federal of Fire Chaplains, 2005), 239.
[158] Staufer, Duncan, and Lotz, 239.
[159] Staufer, Duncan, and Lotz, 240.

Religion and Art

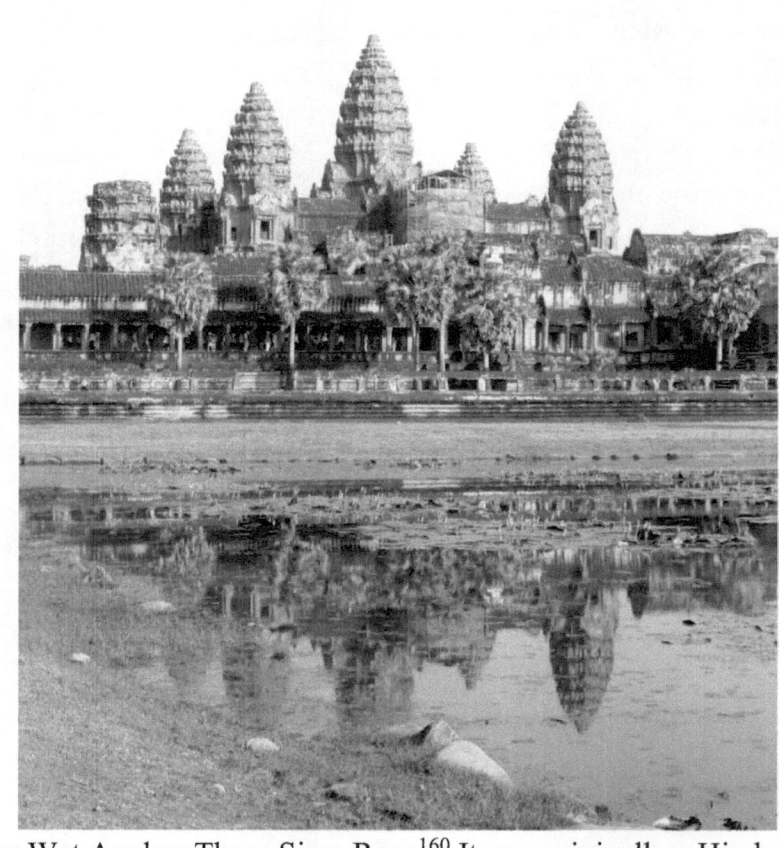

Angkor Wat Angkor Thom Siem Reap[160] It was originally a Hindu temple but was transformed into a Buddhist temple.

---

[160] icon0 com, *Angkor Wat, Angkor Thom, Siem Reap, Cambodia*, Digital Image, *PublicDomainPictures.net*, accessed May 30, 2023, https://www.publicdomainpictures.net/en/view-image.php?image=336690&picture=angkor-wat-angkor-thom-siem-reap.

Discussion Questions for lessons, book, and Bible studies

1. Describe key arts that Buddhists have used to shape their world.
2. Describe some of the Buddhist prohibitions on art.
3. Describe some Buddhist wedding and funeral customs.
4. Describe one way that you have seen Buddhists using the arts to shape the world in your life.
5. Share some thoughts about sharing the gospel with Buddhists.
6. What does the Bible say about the beliefs and actions noted in this chapter?

7

How do other religionists and secular groups use the arts to shape the world?

From Tabernacle to Temple, the Hebrews used the arts to communicate their beliefs about God and to inspire others to adopt them. Their contemporaries in Assyria, Babylon, and Egypt did the same. Alexander, Caesar, and Napoleon followed suit, using music and other arts to cow their enemies, hearten their friends, and persuade the undecided. It is no different today.

Along the outer loop of the Beltway (Interstate 495) north of Washington DC, westbound drivers approaching the Connecticut Avenue exit are greeted by a remarkable sight - the white spires of the Temple of the Washington DC Church of Jesus Christ of the Latter-Day Saints (LDS). The view is inspiring, and one wants to go to the temple just to see the rest of it. The Mormons have built or are building hundreds of impressive temples and churches throughout the globe, from Aba, Nigeria to Winnepeg, Canada. Each temple attracts onlookers with its beauty, confers a favorable impression of the Mormon faith, and may even encourage people to join the church.

The Mormon Tabernacle Choir is renowned for its magnificent music, performing for Mormon and non-Mormon audiences all over the world. The choir is a marvelous ambassador for the LDS church, with fresh faces and beautiful voices communicating joy, sadness, and power through their songs. Painting is also prominent in the LDS church, including both religious and secular topics. The famous work *The Prayer at Valley Forge* was painted by the Mormon artist Arnold Friberg (1913-2010). The LDS church uses statuary, drama, and even dancing. There are many other examples; Mormons use the arts extensively to shape the world.

Art is also prominent in traditional African religions. Musicians and dancers create rhythms that grab the heart and move the feet. Sculptors make figurines and statues to portray spirits, enhance fertility, and bring good luck. Villagers have body markings including tattoos and cicatrices (decorative scars). Facial marks may indicate tribal allegiance, or suggest virility, ferocity, or skill. Natives believe that body markings near genitalia increase sexual pleasure.[161] Traditional African art highlights figures, often of stone, bronze, or terra cotta. Many portray normal humans, but others are phallic symbols. These peoples use such figurines in religious, healing, marriage, and other rituals to shape their world.

Modern pagans also use the arts to shape their world. Music has been culturally associated with witchcraft, and pagan musicians have modified and continued this tradition. "Witch camps" include drumming, dance, and artistic rituals.[162] Ritual dance helps worshippers achieve a state of emotional ecstasy, similar to the Whirling Dervishes.[163] Figurines and symbols play an important role in a wide variety of pagan practices. Some pagans borrow ritual practices from Native American and other

---

[161] Geoffrey Parrinder, *Sexual Morality in the World's Religions* (Oxford, England.: Oneworld Publications, 1996), 136-137.
[162] Helen A. Berger, ed., *Witchcraft and Magic: Contemporary North America* (Philadelphia, PA.: University of Pennsylvania Press, ©2005), 159.
[163] Sabina Magliocco, *Witching Culture: Folklore and Neo-Paganism in America*, Contemporary Ethnography (Philadelphia, PA.: University of Pennsylvania Press, ©2004), 170.

indigenous peoples; they sometimes use their arts as well. The purpose is to enhance their own religious experience and to shape the world to suit their interests.

Reggae music is a public expression of the Rastafarian religion.[164] Members of the International Society for Krishna Consciousness (ISKCON), also known as Hare Krishnas, chant 16 rounds of 108 prayer beads daily (1,728 chants).[165] Ananda Marga Yoga Society members perform a spiritual dance (*Kiirtan*) before meditating.[166] Although specific practices of ancient mystery religions were shrouded in secrecy, worship of Dionysus (Bacchus) was noted for singing, revelry, sexuality, and darker elements.[167]

Temples hold a vital place in the artistry of many religions. The Wailing Wall in Jerusalem is the sole surviving element of the Jewish Temple and is the holiest place in Judaism today. *Angkor Wat* is a famous temple complex in Cambodia that has passed between Buddhist and Hindu control over the centuries. *Borobudur*, on the Indonesian island of Java, is the largest and most famous Buddhist temple in the world. The Golden Temple of Amritsar, Punjab, is the holiest site of the Sikh religion, and *Shikharji Yatra* is holy to the Jains. Both as tourists and pilgrims, millions of people per year visit these sites, suggesting that religious buildings have an important role in shaping the thoughts of the people, and the world, around them.

---

[164] House, chart 93.
[165] House, chart 65.
[166] House, chart 64.
[167] Edith Hamilton and Steele Savage, *Mythology*, A Mentor Book (New York: New American Library, 1969), 67.

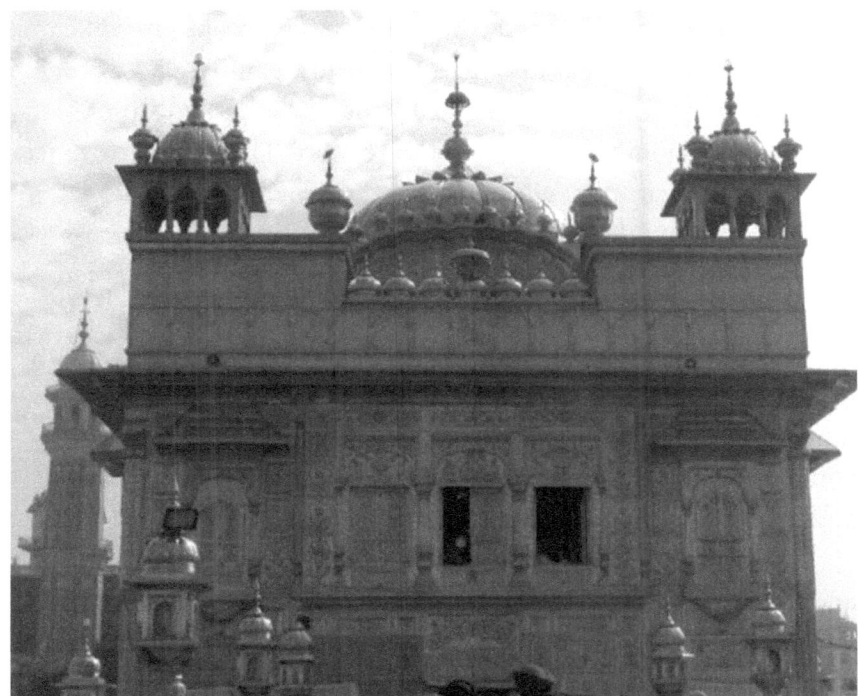

Sikh Temple at Amritsar, India[168]

It is impossible to catalog all the ways that the non-religious people and organizations use the arts to shape the world in their own image, so a few examples will suffice. King Louis XIV's palace at Versailles awed visitors, usually French nobles and foreign statesmen, that Louis (1638-1715) wanted to befriend or cow, with its size and magnificence. Tsar Peter the Great (1682-1721) built the Winter Palace in St. Petersburg for the same purpose, and to demonstrate to the world that Russia was a modern Western nation.

---

[168] Arti Kocchar, *Golden Temple, Amritsar, India*, Online image, *Public Domain Pictures*, accessed April 18, 2023, https://www.publicdomainpictures.net/en/view-image.php?image=22006&picture=golden-temple-amritsar-india.

Religion and Art

Modern marketers use magnificent landscapes to sell cars, adorable animals to sell toys, and beautiful, scantily clad women to sell everything from beer to beds. Music and scents in stores encourage customers to linger and buy more. Using the arts to part people from their money has become a science.

From building the Pyramids to marching armies across Europe, moving muscles together in time to music has enabled groups of men to accomplish feats they could not have otherwise.[169] People listening to music, and especially those moving together to its rhythm, tend to see themselves as part of a moving group, a single organism, rather than distinct individuals. Humans have traditionally used music to initiate a trance state,[170] augment work effectiveness,[171] and consolidate subgroups.[172]

Militaries have perfected the use of music to train, move, and inspire bodies of men. Egyptian soldiers marched to trumpet and drum in 1600 BC, and the Romans did the same 1600 years later.[173] Saracen armies opposing European crusaders had bands with oboes, trumpets, horns, and drums. European bands developed, and by the 19th century Ottoman and Persian bands adopted European instrumentation.[174] Moving in rhythm coordinates actions, whether the loading and volley firing of muskets or the timing of bayonet thrusts. Music enabled marching soldiers to keep in step on long marches and prevented columns of troops compressing their ranks (called "accordioning") into disarray when they stopped and started. Rhythm helps men march

---

[169] William H. McNeill, *Keeping Together in Time: Dance and Drill in Human History* (Cambridge MA: Harvard University Press, 1995), 4.
[170] McNeill, 42.
[171] McNeill, 48.
[172] McNeill, 52.
[173] Max Wade-Matthews, *The History of Musical Instruments and Music-Making: A Complete History of Musical Forms and the Orchestra* (London: Southwater, 2010), 66.
[174] Wade-Matthews, 67.

Other Religions and Art

much farther than they otherwise could. Music builds esprit de corps in armies – at the 1864 Battle of Spotsylvania, Union and Confederate bands competed across the battle lines.[175] Modern armies such as the US Army march to cadences.

Governments use art in propaganda to improve their own image, deface others, and aid in the war effort. Racial and sexual themes are obvious in the American posters from the World Wars noted below. However, racial themes are directed both at the white Germans as well as the darker Japanese. Both images portray the enemy as an ape, blatantly in the World War I poster and more subtly, though the posture, crouch, and arm length, of the Japanese soldier in the World War II poster. Japanese images portray American President Franklin Delano Roosevelt as a Frankenstein-like picture, and several highlight Germany and Japan fighting against the West. German propaganda did not generally picture the Japanese.

---

[175] Wade-Matthews, 67.

Religion and Art

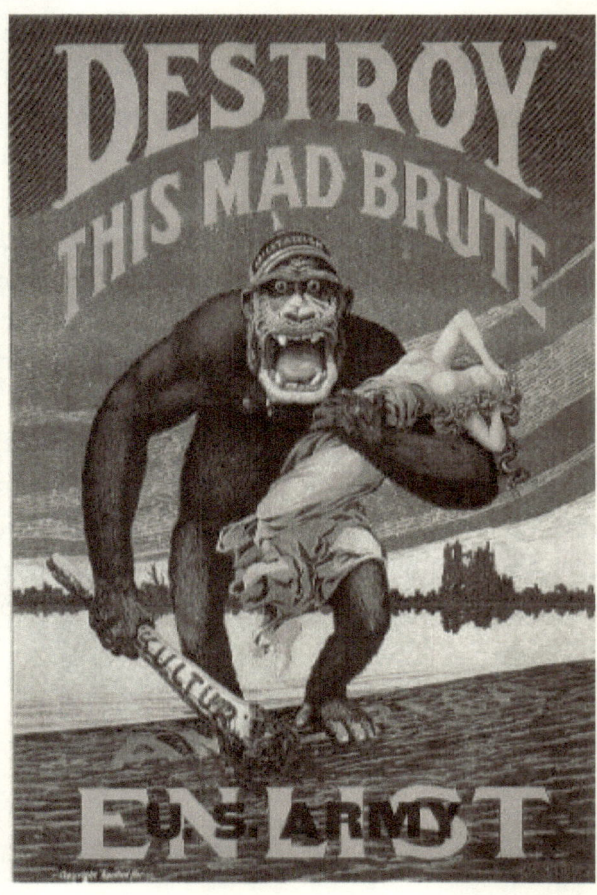

American propaganda poster, World War I[176]

---

[176] Harry Hopps, *Destroy This Mad Brute Enlist - U.S. Army*, 1918, color lithograph, 1918, Washington DC, Library of Congress, https://www.loc.gov/pictures/resource/ppmsca.55871/.

Other Religions and Art

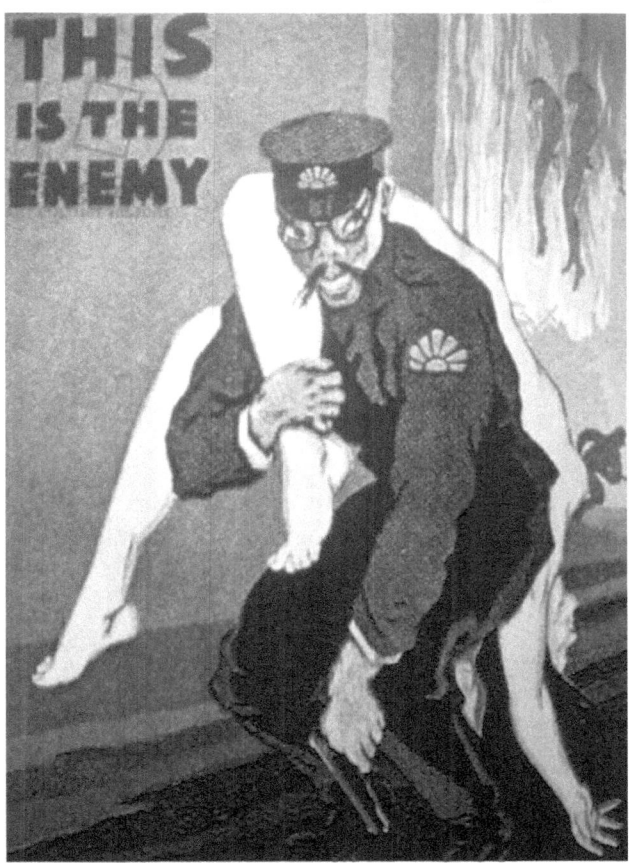

American propaganda poster, World War II[177]

Peacetime pursuits also call for the aid of the arts in shaping society. A famous campaign poster of Barack Obama shows his face in off white, red, and blue, potentially suggesting that if he were elected, he could unite the nation. Art about Trump was often negative, such as a piece with him wearing a swastika over his heart. Corporations sometimes make and distribute images which could be considered propaganda. More often though, in my

---

[177] United States War Department, *This Is the Enemy*, 1943, Online Image, *Wikimedia Commons*, 1943, https://commons.wikimedia.org/wiki/File:US_propaganda_Japanese_enemy.jpg.

experience, people and organizations who dislike a certain corporation will produce propaganda against their foe. Modern social media is replete with videos, memes, and other artistic devises aimed to discredit or destroy anyone the creator does not like.

Discussion Questions for lessons, book, and Bible studies

1. Describe key arts that members of other religions and philosophies have used to shape their world.
2. Describe some prohibitions on art that you see in the secular and non-Christian world.
3. Describe how you see governments and other entities using propaganda to shape the world.
4. Describe one way that you have seen members of other religions and philosophies using the arts to shape the world in your life.
5. Share some thoughts about sharing the gospel with people from atheist, Marxist, and otherwise secular worldviews.
6. What does the Bible say about the beliefs and actions noted in this chapter?

WHAT IS THE BIBLICAL BASIS FOR USING THE ARTS IN CHRISTIAN MINISTRY?

In his book *Art and the Bible*, Francis Schaeffer addresses the question of whether the arts should be used in the Church, and if so, how much. He frames his answer in terms of the fall and restoration of man. Ultimate restoration from the Fall can only come in eternity and through the work of Jesus Christ, but partial restoration is available now. Quoting Francis Bacon, Schaeffer writes "man by the Fall fell at the same time from his state of innocence and his dominion over nature. Both losses, however, can even in this life be in some part repaired; the former by religion and faith and the latter by the arts and sciences."[178]

Commentators rejecting the use of art by the Church have used the Bible to support their position. They often cite the second commandment in the Ten Commandments (Exodus 20:4-5):

> Thou shalt not make unto thee any graven image, or any likeness of anything that is in heaven above, or that is in the earth beneath, or that is in the water under the earth, thou shalt not bow down thyself to them, nor serve them: for I the LORD thy God am a jealous God, visiting the iniquity of the fathers upon the children unto the third and fourth generations of them that hate me.

---

[178] Schaeffer, 18.

Over the past 3,200 years, many followers of Jehovah, whether Hebrew or Christian, have interpreted this passage as forbidding art. Leviticus 26:1 seems to agree, saying "Ye shall make you no idols nor graven image, neither rear you up a standing image, neither shall ye set up any image of stone in your land, to bow down unto it: for I am the LORD your God." These texts seem to forbid images of any kind, whether paintings, sculptures, or any other representation of nature.

A logical conclusion of these passages is that neither Jews nor Christians are allowed to produce any art, except perhaps music. From the iconoclastic reign of Leo III (675-741) to that of the Protestant Reformation and until the present day, some Christians have denied themselves the freedom to participate in the arts. Even dedicated followers of Jesus who consider themselves "forward-thinking" have been iconoclasts.

A look at other portions of the Old Testament, however, belies this interpretation. During Israel's journey through the Sinai Desert, God told them to build a tabernacle; a sacred space where He would dwell among them. The Lord personally gave them the exact design that He wanted them to use (Exodus 25-27) and commissioned the finest craftsmen among the people to lead the work (Exodus 31:1-6). He also directed the style and construction of the priest's garments and other items used in worship. What did God tell the Israelites to make? (1) cherubim (angels) (Exodus 25:18); (2) almond branches and blossoms (Exodus 25:31-33); and (3) blue, purple and scarlet pomegranates (Exodus 28:33).

Note that God told His people to make replicas of spiritual creatures (angels) as well as natural plants. In building the Temple and its accoutrements, the Lord commanded Israel to produce the following (1 Chronicles 28:11, 12,19): (1) cherubim (2 Chronicles 3:7); (2) oxen holding up a 10,000-gallon bowl (2 Chronicles 4:3-4); (3) lilies (2 Chronicles 4:5); (4) lions (1 Kings 7:29); and (5) palm trees and flowers (1 Kings 6:29).

Religion and Art

We see, therefore, that God Himself ordered His people to produce art for the Tabernacle and Temple. He included religious figures, natural figures, and even unnatural figures (blue pomegranates). Secular buildings, such as Solomon's palace, used art (1 Kings 10:18-20). Art was to help the people to worship the true God but was not to be the object of worship itself. The problem addressed in the Ten Commandments is not art per se, but rather the misuse of it. The Lord forbids bowing down and worshipping anything but Himself, and art can lead to idolatry, but art can also be used to communicate Him more effectively.

Music, dance, and its associated ecstasy was a part of being recognized as a prophet in the early kingdom of ancient Israel. After Samuel anointed Saul as king of Israel, he sent Saul to a group of prophets who were prophesying with "harp, tambourine, flute, and lyre" (1 Samuel 10:5-10). The Spirit of God came mightily upon Saul, he was "changed into another man", and he began to prophesy. The people then recognized Saul as a prophet (1 Samuel 10:11-13), which was visible evidence of God's anointing, and he was shortly thereafter recognized as king. King David also had a time of religious ecstasy, dancing before the Lord with all his might while wearing only his undergarments (2 Samuel 6:14-15, 20). The Old Testament does not record whether or not later kings of Israel and Judah had similar experiences. Perhaps the divine anointing, as evidenced by ecstatic religious experiences as well as the testimony of Samuel, provided legitimacy to the earliest Hebrew kings in the absence of a more traditional source of legitimacy, a royal heritage.

Jesus used art, the bronze image of the snake on the pole (John 3:14-15), to describe the fate of the Son of Man. Ezekiel acted out the siege and conquest of Jerusalem by the Babylonians (Ezekiel 4:1-3). The Song of Solomon is a romantic description of love between a man and a woman but has also been interpreted as an illustration of the relationship between Christ and the Church.

Biblical Basis for Art

David used his poetry, singing, and instrument building and playing as an act of worship.[179] He was famous for dance, as was Miriam before him (Exodus 15:20). Singers played a vital role in the Hebrew religion throughout the history of Israel. The Canticles, hymns taken from the Bible but not from the Psalms, abound in the musical history of Israel.[180]

1. First Song of Moses (Exodus 15:1-19)
2. Second Song of Moses (Deuteronomy 32:1-43)
3. Prayer of Hannah (1 Samuel 2:1-10)
4. Prayer of Habakkuk (Habakkuk 3:1-19)
5. Prayer of Isaiah (Isaiah 26:9-20)
6. Prayer of Hezekiah (Isaiah 38:10-20)
7. Prayer of Jonah (Jonah 2:2-9)
8. Prayer of the Three Holy Children (Daniel 3:26-56)
9. Song of the Three Holy Children (Daniel 3:57-88)
10. Song of the Theotokos (the Magnificat: Luke 1:46-55)
11. Song of Zacharias (the Benedictus Luke 1:68-79)
12. Prayer of Simeon (Nunc Dimittis Luke 2:29-32)

On balance, therefore, we see that the Bible promotes art rather than condemning it. Architecture, dance, drama, music, painting, and sculpture are integral to the full understanding of God and the world. The Lord is the consummate artist, and He gave man the ability to create art in His creation. Only the misuse of art, worshipping what the hands of man has made, is forbidden.

There is another significant objection to the use of art in the church. Paul tells his readers in Philippi to focus their attention on "whatever is true, whatever is noble, whatever is right, whatever is pure, whatever is lovely, whatever is admirable – if anything is excellent or praiseworthy - think about such things." (Philippians 4:8) While music, painting, sculpture, literature, and the other arts

---

[179] Schaeffer, 37.
[180] I have included Catholic, Armenian, Orthodox, and other lists of Canticles, as they differ between traditions.

sometimes portray things that are lovely and admirable, often they do not. Picasso's *Guernica* (1937) displays the horror of the Spanish Civil War. The late Medieval genre *Danse Macabre* (Dance of Death) as typified by Pieter Brueghel the Elder's *The Triumph of Death* (1562), is frightening. *Bohemian Rhapsody* (1975) by the rock band Queen, widely considered one of the greatest songs in rock and roll, is nihilistic. It concludes with "nothing really matters, anyone can see, nothing really matters…to me." Hindu sculptures at *Khajuraho* and *Konarak* are celebrated for their portrayal of elicit group sex.[181] Do these facts prohibit Christians from being involved in the arts, or at least limit Christians to producing and consuming only "positive" art? Critics sometimes attack modern "Christian art" as overly sentimental and superficial. Insofar as they are right, is that the best that believers are allowed to do?

No. While believers in God have made magnificent art, the kind that delights the eyes and lifts the spirit, they have also addressed some of the harshest realities of life. David the Poet, a "man after God's own heart" (Acts 13:22), dealt with sin, repentance, cruelty, and death in the Psalms. Ezekiel dramatized the siege and fall of Jerusalem and the destruction of its inhabitants (Ezekiel 4). Jesus' parables such as the Prodigal Son and the Good Samaritan did not gloss over pain and suffering. Subsequent artists from the painter Rafael to the singer Stephen Curtis Chapman have not avoided suffering and evil in their art. Rather, they have portrayed the glory of God despite suffering and evil in their art.

---

[181] Parrinder, 33-34.

Biblical Basis for Art

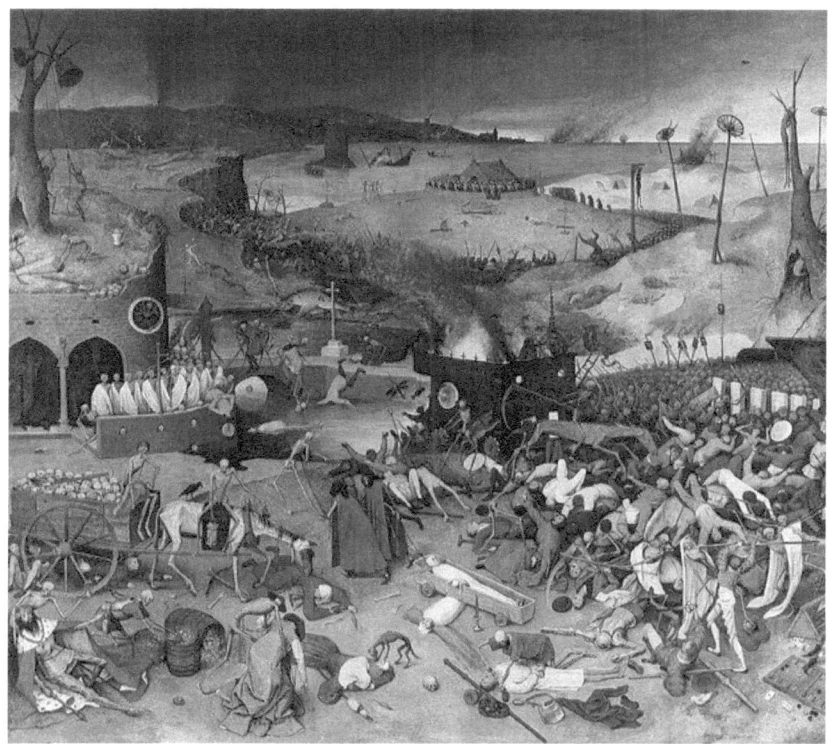

The Triumph of Death by Pieter Bruegel the Elder[182]

Paul's admonition to the church at Philippi was not for them to ignore the harsh realities of life but to see how Christ's work overcomes these realities, healing wounds, soothing suffering, and conquering death. We are not to flee from the pit of human despair. We must look into it and then through it, pulling ourselves and others out of it with the supreme power of Christ. Christian writer C.T. Studd wrote "Some want to live within the sound of church or chapel bell; I want to run a rescue shop, within a yard of hell."[183] The Christian artist will use his or her craft to

---

[182] Pieter Bruegel the Elder, *The Triumph of Death*, 1562, oil on panel, 1562, Madrid, Museo del Prado, https://commons.wikimedia.org/wiki/File:The_Triumph_of_Death_by_Pieter_Bruegel_the_Elder.jpg.
[183] http://www.goodreads.com/author/quotes/3441241.C_T_Studd.

penetrate the realm of darkness with the light of Jesus, bringing sight to the eyes of the blind, and leading them into His glory.

John Newton provides a good example in the classic hymn *Amazing Grace.* His lyrics range from "saved a wretch like me" and "dangers, toils, and snares" to "Grace will lead us home" and "bright shining as the sun." Rembrandt did the same with his painting *Return of the Prodigal.* The sinful but repentant younger son, wearing one shoe and clad in rags, and the bitter, vain, older brother clad in fine robes, reveal two states of human wickedness. Simultaneously, the humility, forgiveness and love of the father overpower the darkness in his children, thus giving hope to the viewers. David plumbs the blackness of his own heart in Psalm 51, but then returns to his only hope, the grace of God. This is the model for Christian art and artists.

In summary, we see that God encourages His followers to engage in arts, but He forbids us from worshipping the products of our own hands or parts of creation. He commands those who believe in Him to explore the depths of hell in their work, whether a physician treating the sickest patients in the poorest places on earth or a writer describing the butchery of Mao, and then lift people out of those depths with His power. Martin Luther captured the might and holiness of the arts well when he said:

> Yes, would to God that I could persuade the rich and the mighty that they would permit the whole Bible to be painted on houses, on the inside and the outside, so that all can see it. That would be a Christian work… If it is not a sin but good to have the image of Christ in my heart, why should it be a sin to have it in my eyes?[184]

---

[184] John Dillenberger, ed., *Martin Luther: Selections from His Writings* (New York: Doubleday, 1962), 495.

Biblical Basis for Art

Pastors, other Christians leaders, and laymen who oppose the visual arts in the local church may wish to consider this statement from the Father of the Reformation.

Religion and Art

Discussion Questions lessons, for book, and Bible studies

1. Describe the arguments for and against the use of the arts in the Church.
2. Describe how God used the arts to give credibility to the priesthood, the monarchy, and other elements in Hebrew life.
3. Describe an example of when you saw someone using the arts to give credibility to someone or something.
4. Share a situation in which you were lifted from brokenness (sadness, anxiety, confusion, or fear) to wholeness in Christ through the use of the arts.
5. What does the Bible say about the beliefs and actions noted in this chapter?

9

HOW CAN CHRISTIANS USE THE ARTS AS OTHERS HAVE TO SHAPE THE WORLD FOR CHRIST?

Christians can transform the styles of art historically used by Muslims into art lifting up Jesus Christ. Believers use architecture and furnishings to shape their world for the Lord. Christian architects of the past intended churches not only to house people for services but also to reveal the interaction between heaven and earth.[185] Christians descended from their Jewish forbears in the arts, and used the Tabernacle and Temple to understand what a building where man meets God looks like.[186] Both Jewish buildings included an area where God actually was, an idea anathema to Muslim thinkers, but which was adopted in the idea of the Eucharist and the altar.

The architecture of the Hagia Sophia inspires awe. Notre Dame in Paris, Mont Saint Michel, the Vatican, and Saint Paul's in London exemplify fine Christian architecture. Non-religious buildings built in the Byzantine style evidence the influence of the Church on architecture. Protestant churches often show beauty in their architectural simplicity.

---

[185] Denis R McNamara, *How to Read Churches: A Crash Course in Ecclesiastical Architecture* (New York: Rizzoli International Publishers; London: Ivy Press, An Imprint of The Quarto Group, 2011), 10.
[186] McNamara, 113.

Religion and Art

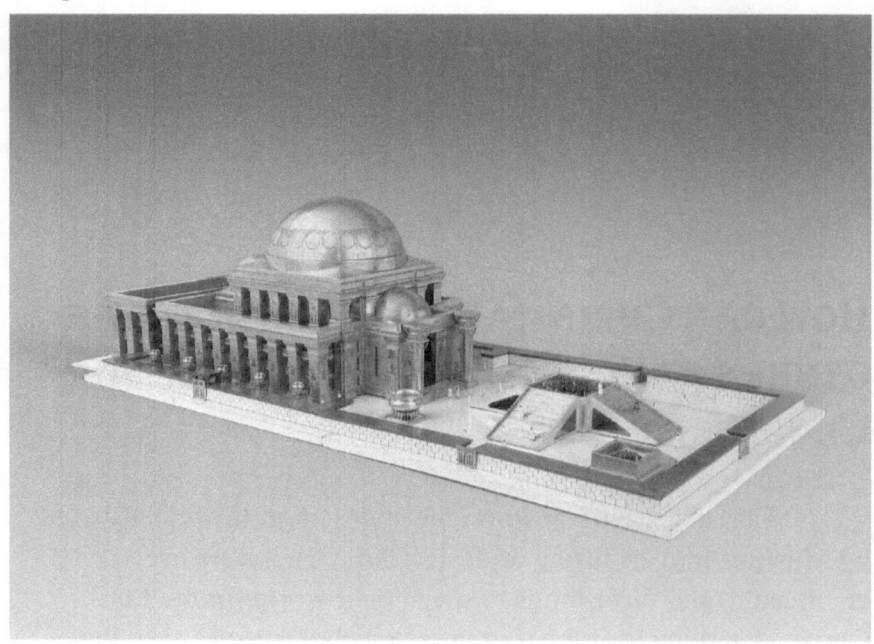

Jewish Temple at the time of King Solomon[187]

Christian workers in cloth make quilts and clothes with Christian themes and do the same with tapestries. This may be especially appropriate for believers in lands with a textile tradition such as Turkey. The instructions that God gave to Moses for the clothing of the high priest are examples of His people using ornate clothing in service and worship (Exodus 28:1-5, Exodus 39).

God's people have glorified Him with poetry since Moses. Modern Christians such as T. S. Eliot have continued the tradition. Dancing, too, has a place in the modern church, just as it did with David three millennia ago (2 Samuel 6:14). The disciples of Mohammad have no monopoly on these types of art, for the God of Abraham, Isaac, and Jacob created all things. Followers of the

---

[187] Messrs. Bartlet and W Spurrier, *Architectural Model of the Temple of King Solomon in Jerusalem*, 1883, Gilded wood, gilded carton pierre; gilded silver, gilded bronze; enamel, 1883, New York, The Met Fifth Avenue in Gallery 554, https://www.metmuseum.org/art/collection/search/786829.

Messiah must use arts traditionally employed by Muslims, such as architecture, tapestry, and verse, to shape the world for Christ.

Just as painting and sculpture, particularly for idols, are prominent in Hindu worship, so Christians have used painting and sculpture to glorify Christ. The Last Supper, the Statue of David, and the Deposition of Christ are illustrious examples. Eastern Orthodox icons also serve to reveal the One God to His people. Many modern Christian painters and sculptors produce beautiful work. Book painting has a long tradition in Christian Europe, with the *Book of Kells* being a prominent example. Such book painting could certainly find wide acceptance today.

From C.S. Lewis to Tim Keller, Christian prose has shaped the contemporary world. J.R.R. Tolkien, Mary Flannery O'Connor, Madeleine L'Engle, and T.D. Jakes have done the same in fiction. And no one can overlook the earth-shattering impact of Christian giants including J.S. Bach, Georg Fridric Handel, and William Shakespeare. Followers of Jesus Christ have dominated arts of all types since the earliest Christians wrote stylized IXOYE on the catacomb walls of Rome.

Stupas contain relics, typically grave sites, of famous Buddhist monks or nuns. In Buddhism they are often places of meditation or even worship. Christians are justly forbidden from worshipping the creature rather than the Creator, but the Scriptures encourage us to remember saints who have gone before (Hebrews 11). When traveling throughout Europe, I have reflected on the lives of our predecessors in the faith such as Thomas Aquinas (1225-1274) and John Knox (1514-1572). Visiting museums, graves, and other important places in their lives, often artistically embellished, can inspire us from their example.

The local church should actively encourage art. Christians, whether in groups or as individuals, can sponsor artists and commission artwork. Christ is Lord over His entire creation, and that includes every person, every living thing, and even every

Religion and Art

substance that He has made. Everything can and should be used for the glory of God.

The next several chapters will highlight many of the ways that the Church, the bride and body of Christ, have used art to shape the world for Him in the past. By remembering what our ancestors did, we can find ideas for shaping the world for Him now and in the future. The story begins in the Roman Empire.

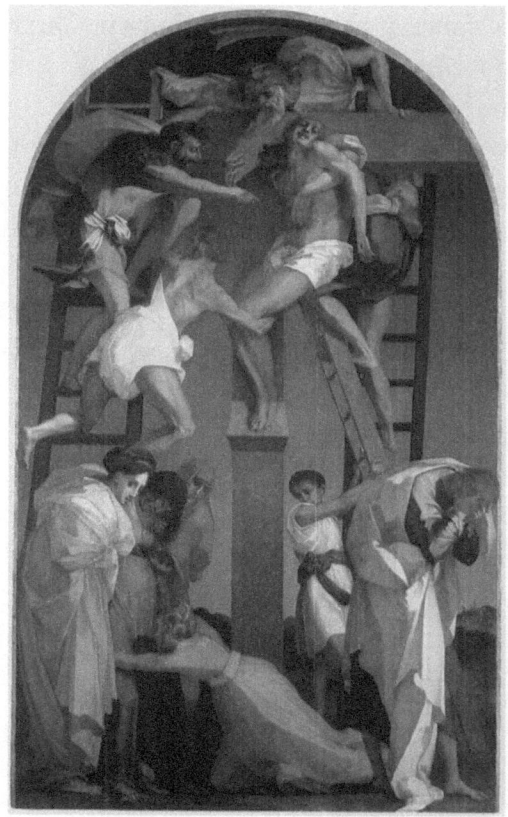

Descent from the Cross[188]

---

[188] Rosso Fiorentino, *Descent from the Cross (Deposition from the Cross)*, 1521, Oil on Panel, 1521, Volterra, Italy, Volterra City Museum and Art Gallery, https://en.wikipedia.org/wiki/Descent_from_the_Cross#/media/File:Rosso_Fiorentino_002.jpg.

Discussion Questions for lessons, book, and Bible studies

1. What was the relationship between Jewish and Christian art in the early church?
2. Name some Christian architecture not mentioned above which has been meaningful to you. If you can, find illustrations online to share with your group. Explain what you like about it. Ask for feedback from them.
3. Name some Christian writings not mentioned above which have been meaningful to you. If you can, find illustrations online to share with your group. Explain what you like about it. Ask for feedback from them.
4. Name some Christian paintings or other visual arts which have been meaningful to you. If you can, find illustrations online to share with your group. Explain what you like about it. Ask for feedback from them.
5. Name some Christian art of any type which has been meaningful to you. If you can, find illustrations online to share with your group. Explain what you like about it. Ask for feedback from them.
6. What does the Bible say about the beliefs and actions noted in this chapter?

10

USING THE ARTS TO SHAPE THE WORLD FOR CHRIST IN THE ROMAN EMPIRE (30-400s)

Cultures since the dawn of time have used space to allocate power. During a tour of Washington DC several years ago, I asked the guide why the Supreme Court building was so grand. He replied that the power of the Supreme Court, or any government, comes from the trust of the citizens to whom that government is responsible. Without trust no government can function or even survive. The Supreme Court building is grand because people coming into the Court must believe that the Court itself is grand, that the law the justices interpret is grand, and that their interpretations of those laws will also be grand.

The use of grandeur as a tool for governing is not new. Ultimately, each person has roughly the same amount of lifespan (70-80 years, give or take), physical strength (no one can bench press 2,000 lbs), size (5-6 ft, 100-300 lbs, give or take), and other physical characteristics. We all drink, eat, sleep, procreate, and handle waste in the same way. Given our similarities, those who would rule over us must have something extraordinary. King Charles III and other monarchs have "royal blood" and historical legitimacy. Constantine had an auspicious birth, an iron will, and martial prowess. Mohammad had a prominent family and

Art use in 30-400s

organizational abilities. With his innovative and pan-Arab faith, and after his military and political victories, he also had religious legitimacy. John F. Kennedy became president with his own good looks, charisma, and his father's fortune.

Great historical buildings and gardens, like Louis XIV Versailles, Red Square, and the Forbidden City help rulers or would-be rulers impress or cow the public, the court, and potential rivals to power. Impressive and expensive furnishings add to the effect. Cathedrals do the same.

The Jewish Temple reveals how architecture and furnishings confer power.[189] The Temple emphasized the might of God by including an area strictly for Him, the Holy of Holies, and forbidding anyone to enter it at any time. The only exception was the High Priest, who could enter the Holy of Holies once per year under strictly controlled conditions (Leviticus 16:1-34).[190] These restrictions taught the Hebrews that God was holy, that He was glorious, and that He was in the Temple. The Temple had power insofar as God dwelled there (Ezekiel 10:18). It also had power due to the peoples' perception that God dwelled there. In every religion, at least part of the power of a sacred location lies in the perception that the divine dwells there.[191]

The Temple also assigned social power. The inside of the building, the place closest to God, was exclusively for priests. The presence of the Temple occasioned the Temple tax (Exodus 30:13), which provided wealth, legitimacy, and social power to the religious class.

---

[189] Jeanne Halgren Kilde, *Sacred Power, Sacred Space: An Introduction to Christian Architecture and Worship* (Oxford: Oxford University Press, 2008), 7.
[190] The deaths of Nadab and Abihu, sons of Aaron the High Priest, struck the community of Hebrews. It begged the question of how anyone could come before God and live. Leviticus 16 prescribes how high priests were to carry out these holy duties.
[191] Kilde, 46.

Religion and Art

The inner courtyard was restricted to Jewish men. The middle courtyard held Jewish women and children, and only the outermost area was accessible to Gentiles. Finally, the Temple distributed personal power. Much of the authority enjoyed by the priests in Jewish society derived from their freedom to move between areas in the Temple court, their knowledge of Temple rituals, and the fact that only they were authorized and required to perform temple rituals. Conquering Babylonians (586 BC) and Romans (70 AD) demonstrated their power over the Jews by tearing down the Temple, and the Roman general Pompey exhibited his might by entering the Holy of Holies when his armies took Jerusalem in 63 BC.[192]

The early Church used paintings and icons to communicate their understanding of and love for Christ. The houses of Christians that were used for churches often had fish, bread, and other images that they borrowed from the Jewish culture.[193] The paintings in the Catacombs of Priscilla in Rome featured Christ as the Good Shepherd (c 300).[194] Notably, Christ in this work has the same features as the Roman god Apollo in classical art, just as early Buddhists gave the Buddha Apolline features.[195] From the beginning, early believers have transformed common symbols and images with Christian themes to minister to the world.

After the Edict of Milan (313) which legalized Christianity in the Roman Empire, believers had to decide how to deal with the

---

[192] Flavius Josephus, *Josephus: The Complete Works.*, trans. William Whiston (Nashville: Thomas Nelson Inc, 1998) Book 1, Chapter 7, 665-666.
[193] Kilde, 28.
[194] Glaspey 21.
[195] Siddhartha Gautama lived from roughly 560 until 480 BC. Alexander the Great (356-323 BC) conquered the entire Middle East, Persia, and western India (modern Afghanistan and Pakistan) in the last years of his life. Alexander brought Greek thinking, languages, and actions to India, and the Greeks absorbed some Hindu, especially Upanishadic, and Buddhist notions.

non-Christian arts.[196] Theater played a major role in pagan worship in Greece and Rome, and some elements of the Church tried to ban dancing, mysteries, the wearing of the dress (attire) of the opposite gender, and the masks of comedies and tragedies.[197] Rather than banning them, other Christians co-opted pagan festivals, temples, sanctuaries and plays for Christian ministry. The Byzantine *Christos Paschon (Passion of Christ)* is a play that borrows half of its text from dramas written by the pagan Euripedes.[198]

Early Christians recognized the power of music and continued many of the Jewish musical traditions. In church and synagogue, the standard liturgy included Scripture reading, teaching, baptism, prayer, fasting, and the singing of psalms and hymns.[199] Jewish cantors who later became Christians, trained to lead music in the synagogues, adapted their skills to their new faith. Writing to the Emperor Trajan (53-117), Pliny the Younger (61-112) noted that Christians gather before dawn on a specified day to sing a hymn, pledge themselves not to commit a crime, and to return later in the day to eat together.[200]

Instrumental music and dancing were associated with pagan ritual, debauchery, and immorality, and thus were forbidden.[201] Aware that the Old Testament promotes instrumental music but concerned about the power of music to incline listeners to sin, some early Christians allegorized the ancient Hebrew passages. The harp became the "active soul", the psaltery was the "pure mind", the ten strings were the "ten nerves".[202]

---

[196] The Edict of Milan did not make Christianity the official religion of Rome. It only guaranteed religious liberty.
[197] John Russell Brown, ed., *The Oxford Illustrated History of Theatre* (New York: Oxford University Press, 2001), 64.
[198] JR Brown, 65.
[199] Wilson-Dickson, 25.
[200] Wilson-Dickson, 28.
[201] Wilson-Dickson, 28.
[202] Wilson-Dickson, 39.

Religion and Art

The pagan Irish initially resisted St. Patrick's (c.387-c.460) message of Christ. He preached the word of God, adapted as best he could to their culture, but still the soil was hard. Turning to the arts, Patrick combined the Latin cross with the Celtic sun, developing the Celtic cross. In the famous legend about shamrock, Patrick used the three-leaf clover to teach Irish villagers about the Trinity. Preached words, visual symbols, Christianized Irish ritual, and ultimately the work of the Holy Spirit led to a marvelous harvest.[203]

---

[203] J. Scott McElroy, *Creative Church Handbook: Releasing the Power of the Arts in Your Congregation* (Downers Grove, IL: IVP Books, 2015), 256-7.

Discussion Questions for lessons, book, and Bible studies

1. How did the Christians use and adapt Jewish art to understand and communicate their new faith?
2. How did the Christians use and adapt Greek and Roman art to understand and communicate their new faith?
3. How does space connote and distribute power and wealth in your home, your church, and your community?
4. How do restrictions on the arts today compare with restrictions in the ancient world?
5. What art and symbols have been repurposed for Christian use in the past? What about today?
6. What art and symbols must Christians reclaim from their use in the world?
7. What does the Bible say about the beliefs and actions noted in this chapter?

11

USING THE ARTS TO SHAPE THE WORLD FOR CHRIST IN THE MIDDLE AGES (500s-1300s)

People often have their minds fixed on the near future, worrying about what is to come. We occasionally center our thoughts on the here and now, and as we age, we increasingly think about the past, for good and for ill. Rarely, however, do we take time to consider the eternal. One of the most important functions of religious ritual is to focus attention on what is cosmically significant.[204] Especially in the Middle Ages, art and architecture functioned as part of ritual practice.

The *Book of Kells* (c 550) is an outstanding example of art that encourages worship. The book is a Latin translation of the Four Gospels from the monastery at Kells, Ireland. While readers study the words of God, the book's rich illustrations delight viewers with complexity and beauty.[205] The *Lindesfarne Gospels* (c 700) from Northumbria is another classic illuminated manuscript.

Bibles and other literature were extremely expensive and therefore in short supply in the medieval world. As a result, most

---

[204] Kilde, 57.
[205] Glaspey 23-26.

people and even many priests were illiterate. There was no central theological school to train priests and other religious teachers, so Biblical literacy was poor in all classes of European society, including the clergy. Faced with this dilemma, the Church standardized architecture to highlight the glory of God and the sinfulness of man.

First, standardized architecture allowed believers to communicate truths about Christ to churchgoers as well as to the outside world.[206] The generic basilica church, for example, included an atrium (open area near the entrance), a narthex (between the atrium and the nave, and separated from the nave by a railing), a nave (including the center aisle and seating), an ambo (pulpit), and an apse (chapel off the nave).[207] These basilicas sprouted up everywhere, and their design modified the ritual to conform to the intentions of Church leadership. Early in the Middle Ages, for example, the Church chose to emphasize the mystery and power of the Eucharist ritual, and the altar was placed at the extreme visual and aural range of congregants gathered in the nave.[208] This forced the worshipper to seek the blessing and to decode the mystery of the Eucharist. Later, church leaders wanted to focus on the accessibility of God to man, and so moved the altar closer to the congregation. Gothic churches were built and furnished to convey the mystery of the divine, producing visual and tactile effects that would inspire awe in local gentry and peasantry alike. They evoked the power of the divine and of the holy life, often through the skillful manipulation of natural light through stained glass.[209]

---

[206] Kilde, 32.
[207] McNamara, 90.
[208] Kilde, 77.
[209] Kilde, 67-9.

Religion and Art

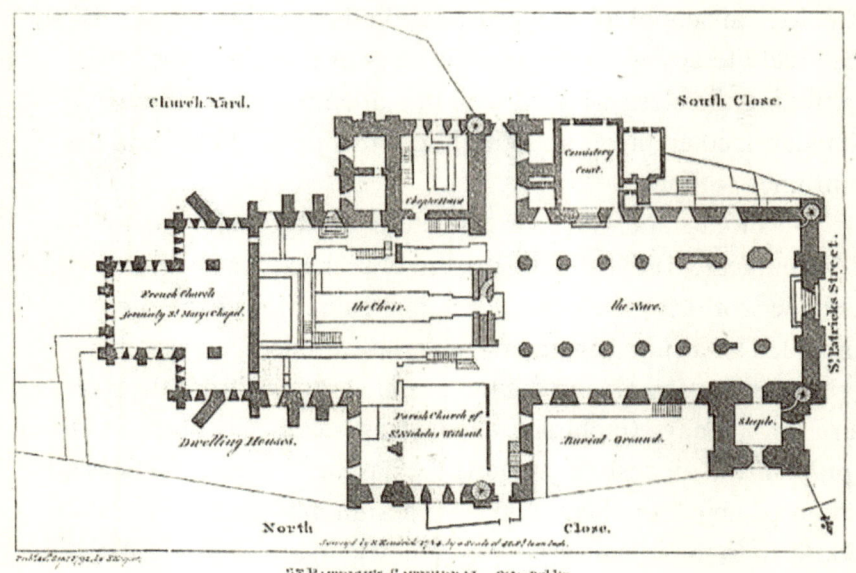

Standard Basilica Design[210]

Second, standardized architecture in cathedrals taught the Bible. As we shall see later, stained glass, paintings, sculptures, music, and other arts, communicated Bible stories and theological truths that both clergy and laity could learn. These works of art would remain with the church day and night and year after year, proclaiming the truths of Christ no matter how good or bad, wise or foolish, the priest or the people proved to be.

Despite this rich tradition, ever since God told Moses at Mount Sinai not to produce any graven images (Exodus 20:4), Christianity and art have been tense brothers. The Byzantine Emperor Leo III (675-741) outlawed Christian imagery and his government destroyed many works of art. Not until the Second Council of Nicaea (787) and the accession of Empress Eirene (752-

---

[210] Francis Grouse, *Mid 18th Century Plan*, 1794, *Wikimedia Commons*, 1794, https://commons.wikimedia.org/wiki/File:Dublin,_St.Patrick%27s_Cathedral_pl an.jpg.

803) was art reinstated in the Empire. Iconoclasm resurged from 814-843, but art subsequently returned as a vital part of Christian worship.[211]

Part of the tension resulted from people worshipping icons. During Leo's reign, Icons of Christ, Mary, or the saints were kissed, caressed, wreathed in garlands, and adorned with spices. Icons were godparents for children, defenders of cities, and presiding officials at races. People scraped the pigments off icons to add to drinks for their supposed healing powers.[212] Religious leaders emphasized the symbolic nature of the icons, but the populace made little distinction between the image and the personage represented there.[213]

One wonders how much Christian iconoclasm was encouraged by Muslim iconoclasm. By the time of Leo's death, Islam had spread from Persia to Spain. Constantinople had been saved by a hair from Muslim armies (674-678 and 717-718). Christian chroniclers of the day wondered why God gave them so often into the hands of their enemies. Undoubtedly many felt that Christian idolatry was to blame. Leo certainly believed that image worship was the main obstacle preventing Muslims and Jews from coming to Christ.[214]

Some of the modern papal accoutrements originated in the Middle Ages. Each Pope wears a "ring of the fisherman" featuring St. Peter in the center and the name of the current pope (the wearer) around the outside. The papal crozier, a staff shaped like a shepherd's crook, is another example. Both serve to differentiate

---

[211] MP Brown, 73-74.
[212] Ted Byfield and Paul Stanway, eds., *The Christians: Their First Two Thousand Years*, vol. 6, *The Quest for the City A.D. 740 to 1100* (Canada: Christian History Project, Inc., 2004), 118.
[213] This behavior is similar to how Hindus treat their idols and is a strong argument for iconoclasm. The heart of man is desperately wicked and wants to worship something.
[214] Byfield and Stanway, 121.

the Pope from other Catholic leaders and confirm his authority over the faithful.

Theater was important in churches during the Middle Ages. Secular Greek and Roman plays remained popular in Europe throughout the period, but the medieval church nurtured the theater, using it for training in theology as well as political advantage.[215] Liturgical dramas based on Bible stories, or the lives of saints, were very popular. *The Holy Resurrection* (1179) and Hildegard of Bingen's (1098-1179) *Order of Virtues* (1140s) are famous examples.[216] *Ordo Virtutum* was the first musical drama in history.[217] The stage, the set, the costumes, and the actors provided a powerful way to teach Bible truths to illiterate people.

Christians did not begin to write down the music that they used in worship until the 6th and 7th centuries.[218] The Gregorian chants, named after Pope Gregory (540-604), are the most famous example of Christian music in the Middle Ages. Initially associated with the monastic movement, these chants were monophonic (no harmony, only melody) and acapella, emphasizing power, purity, and simplicity to their hearers. Antiphones, a response by a choir or congregation to a psalm, and cantillation, the modulation of the speaking voice, developed as important musical features. The schedule in Benedictine monasteries was arranged so that all 150 psalms would be sung each week.[219] Benedict devoted many hours throughout each morning and evening for music.[220] Gregorian chants, well suited to the superb acoustics of many cathedrals, quickly made their way into mainstream Catholic life. Transported

---

[215] JR Brown, 72, 109, 220.
[216] JR Brown, 68-69.
[217] Glaspey, 31.
[218] Wilson-Dickson, 25.
[219] Wilson-Dickson, 33.
[220] Saint Benedict, *The Rule of Saint Benedict*, Vintage Spiritual Classics (NY: Random House, 1981).

to the heavens with dazzling architecture and magnificent music, peasants and nobles shared a powerful worship experience.

Expanding upon earlier Greek thought, medieval Christians such as the Roman philosopher Boethius (480-524) identified three types of music. The Music of the Universe (Spheres, *musica mundana*) was the natural music related to mathematics and resonant in all creation. *Musica Humana* was music created by people. M*usica instrumentis constituta* was music created by instruments.[221] Mankind's task was to make music that harmonized with the Music of the Spheres. This understanding of music was influential among Christians and even among non-Christians for a thousand years.

Monks often served as musicians in the medieval Church. As music was a major focus in monastic life, they devised methods of writing down music so that it could be standardized, adapted to new instruments, and exported to other places. Guido d'Arezzo (991-1050) was an Italian monk who wrote the *Micrologus*, which included staff notation and the do–re–mi–fa–so–la method of teaching singing.[222] Musical notation invented in the Church developed into the Western Classical Musical tradition.

Polyphony was another medieval advance in music. Chanting in unison had become singing a single line of melody. However, the limitations of human vocal range and ability to hold notes had restricted the amount of ornamentation which could be added to a Gregorian chant. Directors split choirs into parts to sing different sections of the chant, and later added differing melodies which the choir sections, based on vocal range, would sing simultaneously. The Gregorian monophony grew into polyphony - two, three, and even four melodies being sung together and harmonizing with each other.[223] Modern four-part music, including

---

[221] Wilson-Dickson, 40.
[222] Wilson-Dickson, 44.
[223] Wilson-Dickson, 49.

Religion and Art

soprano, alto, tenor, and bass lines, springs from this fountainhead. Adding the voice types for women (soprano, mezzo-soprano, contralto) and men (countertenor, tenor, baritone, and bass) provides more diversity, complexity, and beauty. When combined with instrumental music from a variety of instruments, the possibilities for musical grandeur were, and are, endless.

However, polyphony was controversial. Charles de Ligny (1488-1530) was arrested in the pub Fleur de Lys in London in 1605 because he possessed a copy of polyphonic choral music by William Byrd.[224] Bishop John of Salisbury (1120-1180) argued that the "effete emotings" of polyphonic singers "can more easily occasion titillation between the legs than a sense of devotion in the brain." The "Angelic Doctor" Thomas Aquinas (1225-1274) contended that polyphonic music might suit God and the angels but was not appropriate for mortal flesh.[225] Pope John XXII's papal bull (1324) discouraged polyphony. But despite the controversy, musical innovation endured.

---

[224] The Economist, Dona nobis pacem, 22 Dec 2018 to 4 JAN 2019, London, England, 39
[225] The Economist, Dona nobis pacem, 22 Dec 2018 to 4 JAN 2019, London, England, 39

Art use in 500s -1300s

Discussion Questions for lessons, book, and Bible studies

1. How and why did architecture change during the Middle Ages?
2. What is iconoclasm, and why did it exert such an impact against the arts?
3. How and why did music change during the Middle Ages?
4. How did many Christian leaders in the Middle Ages view theater?
5. How did the monastic movement influence music?
6. What is your opinion about the ornate Catholic cathedrals?
7. What does the Bible say about the beliefs and actions noted in this chapter?

12

USING THE ARTS TO SHAPE THE WORLD FOR CHRIST IN THE RENAISSANCE AND REFORMATION (1300s-1600s)

Sculpture and art are especially helpful to teach illiterate worshippers Biblical truths.[226] Michelangelo's *Pieta*, showing Christ's body in the lap of Mary His mother, invites viewers to join in her grief.[227] Leonardo Da Vinci (1452-1519) placed his characters on one side of the table in *The Last Supper* (1495-1498), beckoning the viewer to observe the proceedings or even to step into the picture. Imaginatively entering a scene helped lay worshippers perceive extraordinary access to spiritual power.[228]

The earliest Catholic services emphasized the Eucharist. Under the influence of the Reformation, the Council of Trent (1545-1563) increased the importance of preaching in Mass relative to the Eucharist. However, they discouraged the use of music. While medieval Christendom emphasized the glory of God and the mystery of the Eucharist, renaissance Christendom in this period emphasized the mind. Sculpture and art after the Reformation served to stir the intellect in its search for God.[229]

---

[226] Kilde, 82.
[227] MP Brown, 221.
[228] Kilde, 88.
[229] Kilde, 100, 108.

Art use in 1300s – 1600s

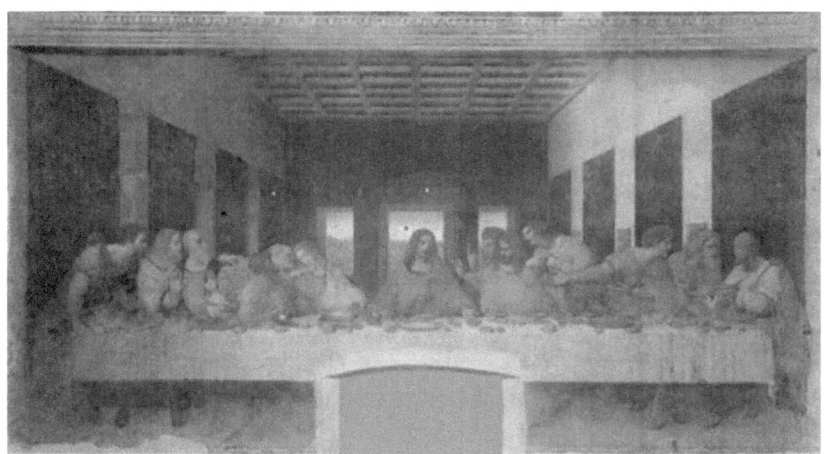

Last Supper, Leonardo Da Vinci, Chiesa di Santa Maria delle Grazie, Milan, Italy[230]

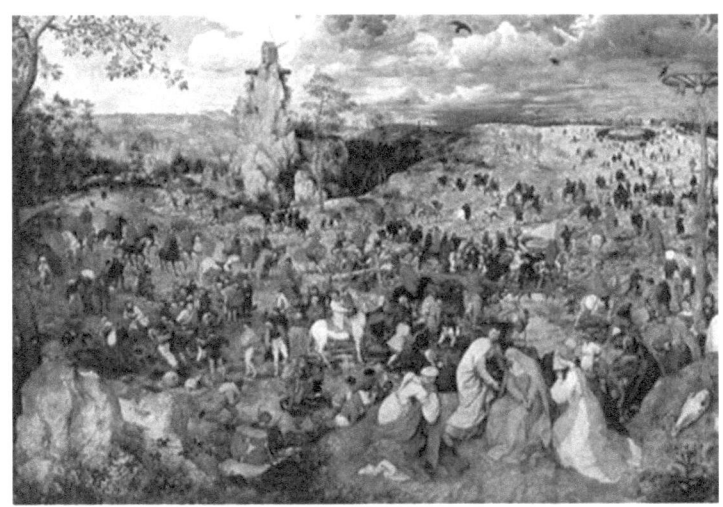

The Procession to Calvary[231]

---

[230] Leonardo da Vinci, *The Last Supper*, 1498, tempera on gesso, pitch and mastic, 1498, Santa Maria delle Grazie Church, https://commons.wikimedia.org/wiki/File:Leonardo_da_Vinci_(1452-1519)_-_The_Last_Supper_(1495-1498).jpg.

[231] Pieter Brueghel the Elder, *The Procession to Calvary*, 1564, Oil on panel, 1564, Vienna, Kunsthistorisches Museum, https://en.wikipedia.org/wiki/The_Procession_to_Calvary_(Bruegel).

Pieter Brueghel's (1525-1569) *The Procession to Calvary* challenges the viewer to find Jesus amidst a throng of people oblivious to His agony, and then challenges them to consider their own oblivion to the work of God. *Agnus Dei (Lamb of God)*, by Francisco De Zurbaran (1598-1664), pictures a lamb, legs bound for slaughter, lying on a dark background. It is a potent and painful image of what Almighty God sacrificed for us.

The theater was still controversial. Samuel Wesley delivered his *Sermon Preached Before the Society for the Reformation of Manners* at the St. James's Church in Westminster (1698). In it he exclaimed:

> …our infamous theaters seem to have done more mischief to the faith and morals of the nation than Hobbes; …with as much reason we may exclaim against our plays and interludes as did the zealous fathers against the pagan spectacles, and justly rank those, as they did the others, among those pomps and vanities which our baptism obliges us to renounce and abhor.[232]

Nonetheless, theater was transformed during this era, with innovations in acting, scene design, and playwriting.[233] Much new material appeared, but as in medieval times, the Church often "Christianized" classical tragedy.[234] The Spanish *Mystery of Elche* is a Renaissance liturgical drama performed at Easter which remains popular today.[235] UNESCO named it one of the masterpieces of the Oral and Intangible Heritage of Humanity.

---

[232] Deborah Madden, "Medicine and Moral Reform: The Place of Practical Piety in John Wesley's Art of Physic," *The American Society of Church History* 73, no. 4 (2004): 752.
[233] JR Brown, 107.
[234] JR Brown, 135.
[235] JR Brown, 142.

The Reformation had its own period of iconoclasm.[236] Constantinople, the "impregnable" Christian capital of the Byzantine Empire and iconophile Orthodox Church, fell to the Turks (1453). Muslim armies humbled Hungary (1526) and besieged Vienna (1529). Europe was terrified of the infidel, but his power seemed unstoppable. Simultaneously, the Catholic Church used images in the veneration of saints, a practice the Reformers strongly opposed.

The Reformer Martin Luther (1483-1546) allowed images for education but was always on the lookout for idolatry. This tradition persists in Lutheran churches today. By contrast Martin Bucer (1491-1551), a mentor of John Calvin (1509-1564), wanted all religious images destroyed. As a result, Calvinist churches did away with images. They used stylized writing instead, similar to what Muslims use in mosques.[237] Henry VIII (1491-1547) split from Rome and formed the Anglican Church in the Act of Supremacy (1534). In a burst of anti-Catholic iconoclastic fervor, the English destroyed images, statues, and abbeys.[238]

The *Genevan Psalter*, by Theodore Beza (1519-1605) and Louis Burgeouis (1523-1600), inspired psalters and hymnbooks around the world. The golden age of the Spanish Empire in the 1500s and 1600s coincided with the golden age of Spanish music. Christobal Morales (1500-1553) was a musician and composer in Pope Paul III's entourage. Antonio de Cabezon (1510-1566) made profound contributions to organ music. Giacomo Carissimi (1605-1674) wrote dramatizations of Latin Biblical texts, which later became known as Oratorio.

In all these works, Christians used the arts to experience God for themselves, to introduce others to the Savior, and to shape their culture. The contributions of these artist-saints changed the

---

[236] Kilde, 125-7.
[237] Kilde, 123-124.
[238] Kilde, 125-7.

world. The Western World, and the whole earth, would not be the same had believers not used the arts to shape the world for Christ.

Art use in 1300s – 1600s

Discussion Questions for lessons, book, and Bible studies

1. How did sculpture and other visual arts change during the Renaissance?
2. Why did iconoclasm return to the Church?
3. How did the influence of Islam affect the use of the arts in the European Church?
4. How did the fall of Constantinople impact the Church?
5. What music and instruments are allowed in your church? Which instruments are used?
6. What do you feel is the theme behind *Procession to Calvary*? Why?
7. What does the Bible say about the beliefs and actions noted in this chapter?

13

USING THE ARTS TO SHAPE THE WORLD FOR CHRIST IN THE MODERN ERA (1700s TO TODAY)

The Thirty Years War (1618-1648) marked the last time that religious conflict tore Europe asunder.[239] Skeptics like Voltaire (1694-1778) and Immanuel Kant (1724-1804) questioned the validity of any and all religions, especially in the wake of such tragedies as the Earthquake of Lisbon (1755). As a result, by the mid-1700s, churches found themselves competing for worshippers in a religious marketplace.[240] Early in the modern era, colonial powers saw Christianity, along with "civilization" and "commerce", as the keys to world domination, societal morality, and human progress. By the early 20th century however, science, not faith, seemed to hold the key to perfecting human society. Einsteinian physics and other "hard" sciences were expected to unlock the physical world while Darwinian evolution and Freudian psychology were expected to unlock the secrets of the mind and the potential of humanity. Marxism seemed to hold the key to long term material prosperity and economic equity.

---

[239] Other religio-political conflicts such as the war in Northern Ireland were not Europe-wide, and other Europe-wide conflicts (WW I and II) were not primarily religious.
[240] Kilde, 132.

Art use in 1700s to today

Protestant groups still avoided the visual arts, but now less because of the Catholic and Muslim influences and more from tradition and materialistic thinking. Nineteenth century "Higher Criticism" in Germany attacked the authority of the Bible. Mainline Christian denominations, such as Lutherans, Presbyterians, Methodists, Episcopalians, and others followed, denying the traditional reliability and authority of the Scriptures. Many of these churches were historically amenable to the arts. Conservative Protestants rejected most of the conclusions of "Higher Criticism," retained their faith in the reliability and authority of Scripture, and rejected the visual arts because they became tied to theological liberalism.

Music remained important throughout Christianity, and dance, in some circles, was widespread. Church music like that of Bach transformed but also lengthened services. Such music was often written by local artists and performed by local choirs.[241] Some nineteenth century groups like the Shakers danced long and hard in their worship services.[242]

Johann Sebastian Bach (1685-1750) was a dedicated Lutheran church musician and one of the greatest composers in history. His six Brandenburg Concertos epitomize a master craftsman working for the glory of God for a reasonable wage paid by the local church.[243] Pietist and English Congregational Hymn traditions arose, and John and Charles Wesley started the Methodist movement. George Frideric Handel (1685-1759) wrote the most famous oratorio in history, *The Messiah*, for Easter services. Notably, despite having been born in the same year and living close to one another, Bach and Handel never met.

---

[241] Kilde, 149.
[242] Kilde, 153.
[243] Bach served as organist and concert master. His highest positions were in Kothen and in the St Thomas Church in Leipzig.

Theater remained significant but controversial. Moving pictures transformed the role that drama played in the witness of Christ. For the first time, audiences and performers did not need to come together at the same place and time. Sidney Olcott's silent film *From the Manger to the Cross* (1912) was the first large scale movie portrayal of the story of Jesus. Many more followed, from the epic *The King of Kings* by Cecile B. Demille (1927) to the Biblical Epics *Quo Vadis* (1951), *The Robe* (1953) and *Ben Hur* (1959).[244] Cinematic depictions of Jesus in the past 60 years from *Jesus Christ, Superstar* (1970) to the South African *Son of Man* (2006) make political and racial statements. *Jesus of Nazareth* (1977) and *The Jesus Film* (1979) are more traditional depictions of the Lord. The latter has been translated into over 1000 languages and viewed by almost five billion people.[245] The recent series *Chosen* fleshes out the gospel story with thought provoking but controversial subsidiary characters and story lines.

Music played a faithful handmaid in the revivals of the 19th and 20th centuries. The vocalist Ira Sankey (1840-1908) accompanied the evangelist D.L. Moody (1837-1899) in his powerful crusades. George Beverly Shea (1909-2013) did the same for Billy Graham's (1918-2018) crusades a century later. The Salvation Army, founded by William Booth (1829-1912) used music to advance the Army's work. He wrote "music is to the soul what wind is to the ship."[246] Music is a key part of the Orthodox tradition. Peter Ilyich Tchaikovsky (1840-1893) wrote the *Liturgy of St. John Chrysostom*. Coptic, Ethiopian, and other African musical traditions communicate the gospel in a way that people in these cultures can most readily understand.

---

[244] W. Barnes Tatum, *Jesus at the Movies: A Guide to the First Hundred Years (Revised)*, 3rd ed. (Salem, OR: Polebridge Pr Westar Inst, 2004), 66.
[245] The History of Jesus Film Project, http://www.jesusfilm.org/about/history.html, accessed 15 Aug 2016.
[246] Wilson-Dickson, 140.

Modern churches frequently use art in current ministry. Children's worship, Sunday School, and Vacation Bible School usually have a craft which teaches about the Bible as well as teaching the arts. Congregational worship services provide live music to more than 60% of Americans each week[247] Churches provide more art and education than social services or political involvement.

We have seen that throughout the history of the Church, the people of God have used the arts to shape their world, and the world that followed them, for Jesus Christ. Just as God has gifted believers to accomplish different tasks in the body, so He has provided the full spectrum of artistic skill to His people to shape the world for Christ. What remains is to discuss specifically how the arts can be used.

---

[247] Mark Chaves, "What Do Congregations Do? The Significance of Christian Congregations to American Civic Life," July 2007, http://wordandworld.luthersem.edu/content/pdfs/27-3_What_is_a_Christian/27-3_Chaves.pdf.

Religion and Art

Discussion Questions for lessons, book, and Bible studies

1. How did the Thirty Years War impact the Church, and the arts therein?
2. Describe how tragedy has impacted your Christian faith. How has it impacted others?
3. How did "higher criticism" impact the arts in the Protestant Church?
4. What does it mean that Christianity must compete in the marketplace of ideas?
5. How did music impact the ministries of the great evangelists?
6. What Christian films have you watched? How did they impact your thinking about Christ?
7. What does the Bible say about the beliefs and actions noted in this chapter?

14

HOW DO THE ARTS HELP SHAPE THE WORLD FOR CHRIST? BY TEACHING ETHICS AND MORALITY

In his study *Literature, the Arts, and the Teaching of Ethics*, Wilson Yates identified two ways in which literature and the arts function didactically in moral education. First, they engage, through greater use of the imagination, our intuitive and affective modes of knowing. Second, they provide concrete, narrative experiences (stories) through which we can understand and enter the life and character of moral experience.[248] By inviting us into a play, song, or painting, or by beckoning us to touch a sculpture and thus enter its world, the arts help us personalize moral and ethical struggles.

Consider the story of Susanna and the Elders, based on the apocryphal chapter of Daniel 13. Two elders spy the beautiful Susanna bathing nude. The men demand sex, and when Susanna refuses, they accuse her publicly of adultery. Susanna is about to be put to death, but Daniel questions the elders, who are found guilty of falsely accusing her. The men are executed, and justice is done.

---

[248] Wilson Yates, "Literature, the Arts, and the Teaching of Ethics: The Survey," *The Annual of the Society of Christian Ethics* (1988): 227-228.

Religion and Art

From 1470, many paintings have portrayed this famous story. The painting by Giuseppe Bartolomeo Chiari (1654-1727)[249] shows a naked Susanna leaning away from the elders, her face flush with fear and her hands protecting herself from their advances. Other portrayals have Susanna fully but provocatively clothed and appear to show her negotiating with the elders as a prostitute might.[250] These pictures challenge the viewer to ask who they are in the drama. Are they the lecherous elders, the innocent bather, the not-so-innocent bather, or the one who will deliver her from them? When I show lecture audiences these pictures, I ask members who they identify with. Women almost universally identify with Susanna as a victim. Men more frequently identify with the elders and cast Susanna as a seductress. The contrast is fascinating and makes for provocative discussions. These paintings invoke our wisdom, our folly, our emotions, our reason, and our self-interest as we contemplate these issues of lust, virtue, and justice. The viewers' response is not academic and sterile but cuts to the heart.

---

[249] https://www.bing.com/images/search?view=detailV2&ccid=0N2Yci%2bJ&id=EB8EF0540B32F58CE856BA0D52A5A5BAADD7E268&thid=OIP.0N2Yci-JPTs8m3qjy9VqQwEXDf&q=susanna+and+the+elders&simid=608030138142163524&selectedIndex=60&ajaxhist=0. Accessed 18 Oct 2017

[250] https://www.bing.com/images/search?view=detailV2&ccid=O4EhhYDt&id=7342B02D8357F5ED427A01E3BB05546BD896E037&thid=OIP.O4EhhYDtTUl9gFOdp-cSFgDtEs&q=susanna+and+the+elders&simid=608055332400860467&selectedIndex=8&ajaxhist=0. Accessed 18 Oct 2017

Ethics and Morality

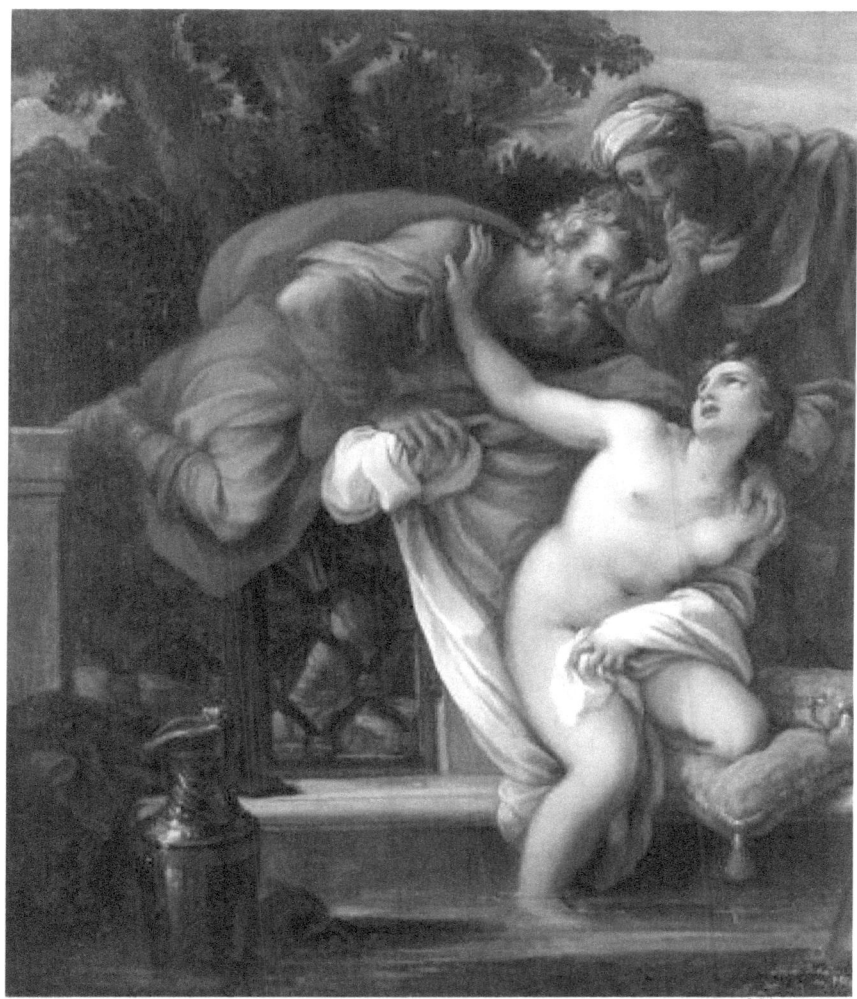

Susanna and the Elders, Chiari, Walters Art Museum[251]

The emotional impact of the arts also improves our long-term memory for lessons learned. Science has long understood that emotional verbal and pictorial stimuli are remembered better than

---

[251] Giuseppe Bartolomeo Chiari, *Susannah and the Elders*, 1727, Oil on canvas, 1727, Baltimore, Walters Art Museum, https://commons.wikimedia.org/wiki/File:Giuseppe_Bartolomeo_Chiari_-_Susannah_and_the_Elders_-_Walters_371880.jpg.

non-emotional stimuli.[252] The best remembered facts are those associated with all the senses (vision, hearing, smell, taste, touch) and with strong emotions. Thus, we are more likely to remember the lessons that we learn through the arts.

The *Return of the Prodigal Son* by Rembrandt contains powerful moral lessons.[253] Viewers usually focus on the younger boy, the sinner who was forgiven and is now embraced by the father. We feel our own pain and the comfort of being restored by our Heavenly Father. Few identify with the older son, locked in his self-righteousness and isolated from the love of his family. Almost no one, though, identifies with the father. He was the aggrieved party in the first place, with a younger son who wished he was dead and an older son who had little use or time for him. Nonetheless, the father is the one who offers forgiveness and love despite what his boys have done. The parable and the painting represent the progression of the Christian life. We begin as the younger brother, sinners receiving the unmerited grace of both God and our fellow Christians. We progress in likeness to Christ, but can too easily become the older brother, spiritually proud and yet bitter about "missing out" on fun and working hard for the Lord without reward. The mature Christian, however, is the father. Though we never wholly outgrow our need for forgiveness and are always in danger of pride and resentment, believers must become like Jesus – wounded, forgotten, and shamed, while loving and forgiving anyway.

---

[252] Susann Eschrich, Thomas F. Munte, and Eckart O. Altenmuller, "Unforgettable Film Music: The Role of Emotion in Episodic Long-Term Memory for Music," *BMC Neuroscience* 9, no. 48 (28 May 2008): 7, accessed March 11, 2016, http://bmcneurosci.biomedcentral.com/articles/10.1186/1471-2202-9-48.
[253] https://www.bing.com/images/search?view=detailV2&ccid=PaGJ3f5z&id=5B2EB15A931B6D07243C3D930974C48721C3C661&thid=OIP.PaGJ3f5zGO0yc3pQOjO9owDaEd&q=return+of+the+prodigal+son&simid=608041184793330853&selectedIndex=0&ajaxhist=0\. Accessed 18 Oct 2017

Pieter Brueghel's (1525-1569) *Procession to Calvary* shows Jesus carrying His cross, small and hard to see in the center of the painting.[254] No one else is really watching; they are all absorbed in their lives and are missing the greatest event in human history. Was Brueghel describing only his own society's reaction to Jesus Christ, or was he describing every society's reaction to Him? Is the modern world much different from the Netherlands in the 16th century?

Some ethical and moral situations are hard to teach since they are not clear cut, but the arts can assist in these areas as well. The practice of medicine is replete with ethical quandaries, such as how to allocate limited resources, how to tell a patient that her case is terminal, and when to finally "pull the plug" at the end of life. There are no easy answers, and the medical staff distance themselves intellectually while emotionally grappling with their own beliefs and fears. Many medical schools and other training programs use role playing to prepare doctors and nurses for such situations. Schools may hire actors to play the roles of the dying patient and concerned family or may use volunteers who have gone through such crises themselves. Students role play in front of professors or other classmates, and everyone involved discusses the scenario afterwards. These exercises not only allow students and faculty to prepare for difficult issues in their future, but also to process such issues from their pasts.

Ethics and morals are changing in medicine. Thirty years ago, physicians gave their personal phone numbers to their patients so that the patient could call anytime and ask any question. Today, such a practice is considered a boundary violation and can end with the physician being punished by the hospital, practice, or state

---

[254]https://www.bing.com/images/search?view=detailV2&ccid=kyt4Rp1p&id=0FD0316561ECED751E5BAA78B0D37E45EF48AB4D&thid=OIP.kyt4Rp1p8R4tFVoOCuIVNw4l6n&q=procession+to+calvary&simid=607997938758978110&selectedIndex=2&ajaxhist=0. Accessed 18 Oct 2017

Religion and Art

medical board. Good doctors gave each patient as much time as they needed, staying late to handle challenging cases. They might give food or even money to a particularly needy patient to get them through hard times. Hugging patients and swapping personal stories was commonplace and even expected. Doctors were part of the lives of their patients, socializing at school programs, church events, and in the market. Such interactions today are discouraged if not forbidden.

In the Christmas story *A Full House*, a doctor delivers a baby in a small country hospital on a snowy Christmas Eve. Since the mother is a recently widowed immigrant, she and her child have no place to go. The doctor takes them to his house to celebrate Christmas with his family and stay as long as they need. Today, he could be fired or have his license revoked.[255] If the mother complained of any perceived impropriety, whether it happened or not, the doctor could be arrested. If, decades later, the mother or child were to have a bad outcome remotely traceable to birth, he could be sued. Her perception, not his intention or action, is all that matters.

Ministers face similar struggles when visiting the sick or providing pastoral care. They also bear burdens of past sins, failures, embarrassments, and frustrations, just as medical professionals do. Bible schools, seminaries, church networks, and even local churches could sponsor role playing workshops periodically for leaders in training and current leaders. Some already do. In her essay "Virtue and Discipline in the Arts," Dr. Carol Reynolds argues that the arts can be a direct path to spiritual virtue.[256]

---

[255] Madeleine L'Engle, *A Full House* (Shaw, 2000).
[256] Reynolds.

Ethics and Morality

Discussion Questions for lessons, book, and Bible studies

1. How do you feel when you see the picture of *Suzanna and the Elders*?
2. Which character do you most identify with in the *Return of the Prodigal Son*? Why?
3. Describe an ethically complicated situation that you have encountered and what you did to resolve it. How could the arts have helped you?
4. Describe a situation in which you have counseled someone else, formally or informally, and how the arts could have helped you.
5. What does the Bible say about the beliefs and actions noted in this chapter?

15

HOW DO THE ARTS HELP SHAPE THE WORLD FOR CHRIST? BY BUILDING COMMUNITIES

People who engage in similar activities tend to congregate. Musicians hang out with other musicians, sports fans cheer with other sports fans, and doctors gather with other doctors. The same is true for visual and other artists. Churches that have music programs meet the communal needs of music-minded people. However, where do the people interested in painting, sculpture, or drama go? Unbelievers who visit a church may enjoy the preaching and the programs but if they do not find a like-minded social group, they are unlikely to stay. If an amateur violinist or flutist wants to use her gifts to the glory of God in her local church, she very likely can. If an amateur painter wants to use his gifts to the glory of God in his local church, he likely cannot.

By making arts ministries available in the local church, pastors and other church leaders can provide the framework around which communities can grow. For example, Christian musicians come together for practices and performances, enjoy church-sponsored and unsponsored activities, and make friends. Leadership is likely volunteer at first, but eventually the church may hire a music minister who provides leadership and pastoral care, including counseling and visitation, to members of the music ministry. As the music program grows, it subdivides into chancel choir, youth choir, children's choirs, orchestra, praise and worship teams, bell choir, and other groups united by their love of music and ministry. Laymen and women lead these smaller groups until and unless they need a professional minister (part or full time) in the ministry.

Our family experience with the arts in churches has been helpful. Coronado Baptist Church in El Paso TX had a choir and praise team led by a music director with instrumental accompanists. At the First Baptist Church of Alexandria VA (FBCA), our chancel choir sang for services and special events, such as Living Christmas Tree and the Southern Baptist Convention (Baltimore, 2014). Our worship teams regularly led on home and overseas mission trips. The bell choir, adult and children, rang the National Anthem at games for the Washington Nationals (baseball) and Washington Wizards (basketball). Meanwhile, our music minister provided the full scope of pastoral care to music participants and their families. FBCA had drama ministries and dance ministries. Many people cited their involvement in these ministries, and in the associated communities, as important reasons for staying at the church. Other churches have used the same paradigm for growing ministries in the other arts, such as painting, sculpture, and poetry.

Germantown Baptist Church (GBC) in Germantown TN, runs a music conservatory program which offers lessons in voice, piano, violin, trumpet, trombone, flute, clarinet, and many other instruments. They also teach classes in ballet and tap dancing. People from all over the community, churched, unchurched, and even from other religions, participate. It was not unusual to see Muslim women bringing their children to GBC for the conservatory. Services at GBC are blessed by professional instrumentalists in the orchestra and a large, well trained worship team and choir. Youth and children's choir sometimes lead music, and periodic musicals bring parents from all over the community.

Religion and Art

Memorial Baptist Church (MBC), a church of about 150 in Beckley WV, has a worship team, bell choir, singing ensemble, and occasional soloists. Children do a special musical program twice a year, which includes music and drama. We also host semiannual hymn sings and Christmas caroling. The MBC Seder supper combines art and ceremony in a powerful ritual during Lent. Youth perform dramas for special occasions and Judgement House at Halloween.

The arts build communities of like-minded people in the local church, and they also help build communities of like-minded people in parachurch organizations. These groups can be local, regional, or even national and have a variety of missions for the Lord's service, including the following:

1. Help local churches and others develop their local arts ministries.
2. Produce higher quality or more expensive art than would be possible for most local congregations.
3. Bring together people who wish to serve God through their art but cannot do so in their local church.
4. Share Christ through the arts to religious and non-religious or even anti-religious communities.

Christians in the Visual Arts (CIVA) is based in Madison, Wisconsin. CIVA members include artists who provide original work to institutions such as colleges and universities and organizations such as churches, galleries, and museums. CIVA matches artists' work with organizations' needs to produce traveling visual arts exhibits for rent. Exhibits are juried to guarantee quality and include historical pieces in addition to original art. CIVA exhibits include painting, photography, sculpture, ceramics, and a wide variety of other forms. Exhibits rent for as little as $800 per month, plus shipping and insurance.[257]

---

[257] "Christians in the Visual Arts," CIVA, accessed 09 Jan 2023, http://civa.org/.

Building Communities

    The Christian Performing Arts Center (CPAC), based in Keller, Texas, produces drama for senior communities, children's homes, hospitals, shelters, churches, schools, parks, malls, festivals, and special events all over the Dallas-Ft Worth (DFW) Metroplex.[258] CPAC also holds summer music and drama camps for children. Similar programs exist across the country.

    DramaShare provides royalty-free Christian drama scripts, skits, sketches, and sermon starters.[259] Memberships are $89/year, and skits and plays can be purchased individually. DramaShare sponsors workshops and conferences to train and encourage churches in the dramatic arts. Finally, DramaShare produces scripts on demand to help churches and other groups and can edit original scripts. Christian Dramas provides similar services.[260]

    The I'll Fly Away Foundation, named after the famous Southern Gospel song, *I'll Fly Away* by Alfred Brumley (1905-1977), encourages music in the home, school, and church. Musical education is a focus. The Foundation sponsors a "You Can Fly" Student Songwriting Workshop and a "You Can Fly" Songwriters Studio.[261]

    Fellowship for the Performing Arts (FPA) is an evangelical non-profit organization which produces professional theater with Christian themes for a diverse audience. FPA has produced critically acclaimed shows such as *The Screwtape Letters*, *The Great Divorce*, *The Most Reluctant Convert*, *The Gospel of Mark*, and *Martin Luther on Trial*. Founded by actor Max McLean, FPA's plays have received outstanding reviews from Los Angeles

---

[258] "CPAC Studios," The Christian Performing Arts Center, accessed 09 Jan 2023, https://cpacstudio.com/.
[259] "Your Christian Drama Resource Center," Drama Share, accessed 09 Jan 2023, https://www.dramashare.org/.
[260] "Welcome to Christian Dramas," Christian Dramas, accessed 09 Jan 2023, http://christiandramas.net/.
[261] "Improving Children's Lives through Music," I'll Fly Away Foundation, accessed 9 Jan 2023, http://illflyawayfoundation.org/.

Religion and Art

to New York.[262] Many Christians in D.C. and other areas invite their non-believing friends. Other parachurch organizations who assist local churches in developing ministries using the arts include Christians in Theater Arts, the International Association of Christian Artists, and Christian Arts Entrepreneurs, Leaders, and Advocates (CAELA).

      These organizations help build communities among artists and empower local churches to begin and build new arts ministries. Local pastors and other church leaders need not feel alone in their attempts to shape their church and communities for Jesus Christ through the arts.

---

[262] "FPA," Fellowship for the Performing Arts, accessed 9 Jan 2023, https://fpatheatre.com/.

Discussion Questions for lessons, book, and Bible studies

1. How have you built community in your home, church, and school or workplace?
2. Could an emphasis on one or more of the arts build community in your life? If so, how?
3. What art-related services would you like to see in your church, such as a music conservatory or an art school?
4. Share an example of how the arts helped build community in an organization in which you were a part.
5. What skills do you have that you could use for an arts ministry in your church?
6. What does the Bible say about the beliefs and actions noted in this chapter?

16

How do the Arts help shape the world for Christ? By revealing the person of God

We have already discussed how Gothic cathedrals used light and Gregorian chants used sound to reveal the glory of God to the people. Such spectacular sights and sounds fill us with a sense of the numinous, something most people rarely feel in the workaday world. Many modern churches, such as the Notre Dame Cathedral in Montreal, do the same. Francisco De Zurbaran's (1598-1664) famous painting *Agnus Dei*, which portrays a lamb fully awake and yet bound for slaughter, poignantly reflects Jesus' sacrifice. The *Stations of the Cross* at the Kreuzberg Monastery in Germany, like the more famous stations of the cross in Jerusalem, help worshipers reenact the Passion of Christ. Sainte Chapelle in Paris overwhelms people with its grandeur, with natural light beaming through large windows between towering walls. Candles flicker and dance, and the cavernous interior amplifies Gregorian chants. As discussed in preceding chapters, Muslims, Hindus, and Buddhists use architecture and other arts to communicate their concept of God, truth, and transcendence.

A systematic way to discover how the arts reveal the person of God is to examine how the arts reveal the person of Jesus Christ.

The Lord made seven famous "I am" statements, and artists have used their talents to illuminate each one.

"I am the Bread of Life (John 6:35)."

An unknown artist painted the *Multiplication of the Bread* in the catacombs of Rome in the 3rd Century A.D. Over a millennium later, Henri Lerambert (1550-1609) produced the *Life of Christ - Multiplication of the loaves and fishes*, for the Church Saint-Merri in Paris (c.1585-90). In 2004, Elizabeth Wang drew a stylized version of the event entitled *Jesus Christ performs the miracle of the loaves and the fish*. Other artists have approached Jesus' role as the bread of life by painting the Lord's Supper or the supper at Emmaus. Still others have simply painted loaves and fish as they might have been at the time. Such works bring these famous Bible stories to life for viewers of all ages and interests from the early church to the modern day. Even more, they reveal the person of God in Jesus Christ.

Many churches celebrate Maunday Thursday, the day when Jesus celebrated the Last Supper, with a Seder supper. A Seder supper is modeled off the Jewish festival of the Passover, commemorating when God struck down all the firstborn of Egypt and freed the Hebrews from slavery. The Christian Seder celebrates the coming of the Messiah using sweet and bitter herbs, salt water, unleavened bread, scripture readings, toasts, and a search for the hidden bread (*afikomen*) to communicate the Gospel to its participants. Dramatizations including Seder suppers communicate Scriptural truths, such as what it means when Jesus says that He is the Bread of Life, in a way beyond the power of many other modalities.

Religion and Art

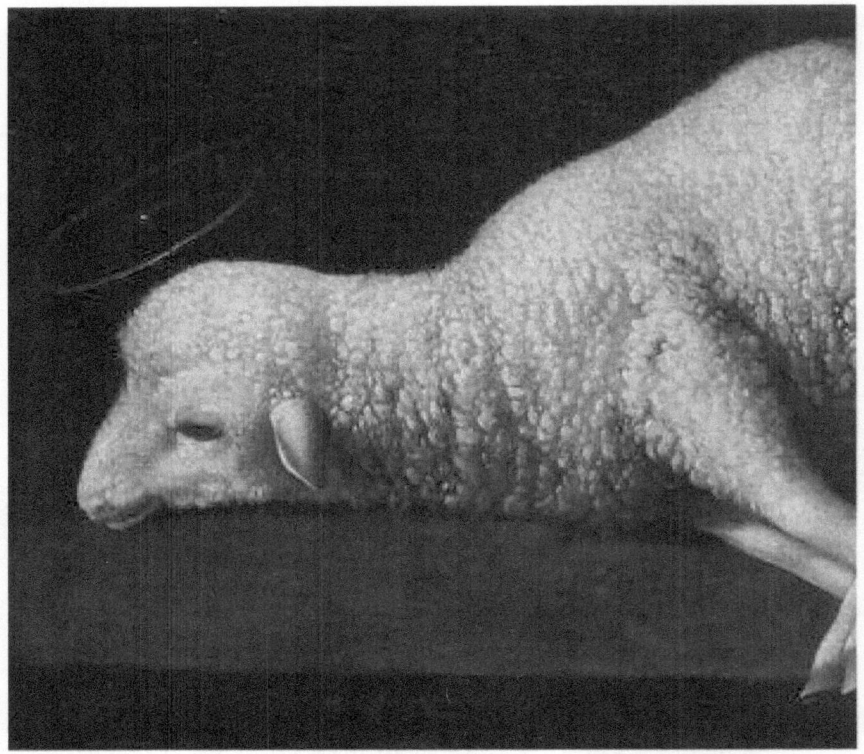

Agnus Dei (The Lamb of God), Francisco de Zurbaran[263]

"I am the Light of the World (John 8:12)."

Stained glass is a favorite way for artists to portray Christ as the light of the world. The Basilica Saint Nazaire, Carcassonne, a UNESCO World Heritage Site in Aude, France and St John's Anglican Church in Sydney, New South Wales, Australia boast two of the most famous examples. Brilliant sunlight illuminates the stained glass to make a spectacular sight. The *Kykkos* Monastery in Cyprus boasts a renowned mural of Christ as the light of the world.

---

[263] Francisco de Zurbaran, *Angus Dei*, 1639, oil on canvas, 1639, Madrid, Real Academia de Bellas Artes de San Fernando,
https://commons.wikimedia.org/wiki/File:Francisco_de_Zurbar%C3%A1n_-_Agnus_Dei_-_Google_Art_Project.jpg.

Painters, sculptors, and poets have also addressed this theme, hoping to communicate the person of God.

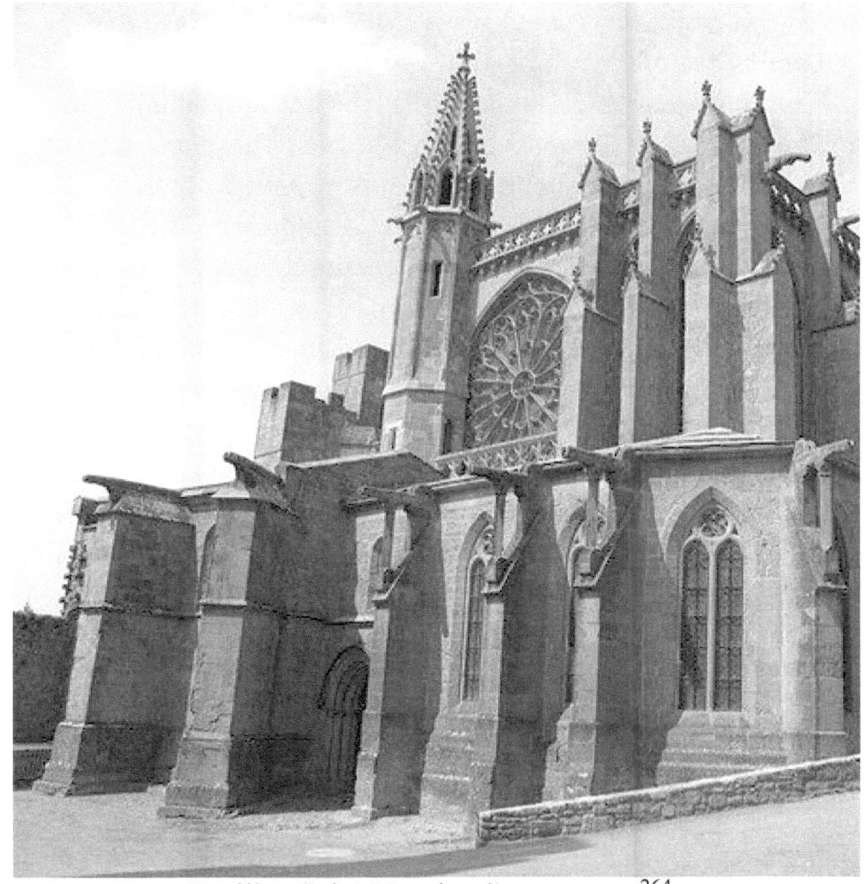

Basilica Saint Nazaire Carcassonne[264]

"I am the Door (John 10:9)."

It is hard to visually portray Jesus as a door, so it is more common to see Him knocking on the door (Revelation 3:20), such

---

[264] MathieuMD, *Basilique Saint-Nazaire in Carcassonne, Seen from South East*, September 26, 2014, Online Image, *Wikimedia Commons*, September 26, 2014, https://upload.wikimedia.org/wikipedia/commons/b/b2/Basilique_Saint-Nazaire_de_Carcassonne_2014-09-26_-_i3121.jpg.

as the painting from Charles S. Anderson (CSA) Design. Malcolm Guite wrote the poem *I am the Door of the Sheepfold* and there are several worship songs about Jesus as the door. *The Savior is Waiting* is one of them.

Judgement House dramatizes repentance, death, judgment, and heaven or hell depending upon whether or not someone accepted Jesus Christ into their life. It is a favorite of youth groups and is usually performed shortly before Halloween. The sponsoring church typically provides counselors after the drama to answer questions and share the plan of salvation. Memorial Baptist Church in Beckley WV has provided Judgement House to its community for several years and has received good feedback, though people coming for the "show" often hail from other local churches rather than being unchurched members of the community. *Judgement House* clearly communicates Christ as the door. Anyone who does not go to the Father through Him will not go at all.

"I am the Good Shepherd (John 10:11)."

Jesus as a Good Shepherd is a favorite motif for visual artists, with the earliest examples being paintings in Roman catacombs and sculptures in early churches. Sir Edward Coley Burne-Jones (1833-1898) did a famous chalk on paper entitled *The Good Shepherd* and Philippe De Champaigne (1602-1674) was one of many who made paintings of the same name. The compassion on Jesus' face when He carries the lost sheep speaks to the compassion He has for us in our most fearful, painful, and confused moments.

Revealing God

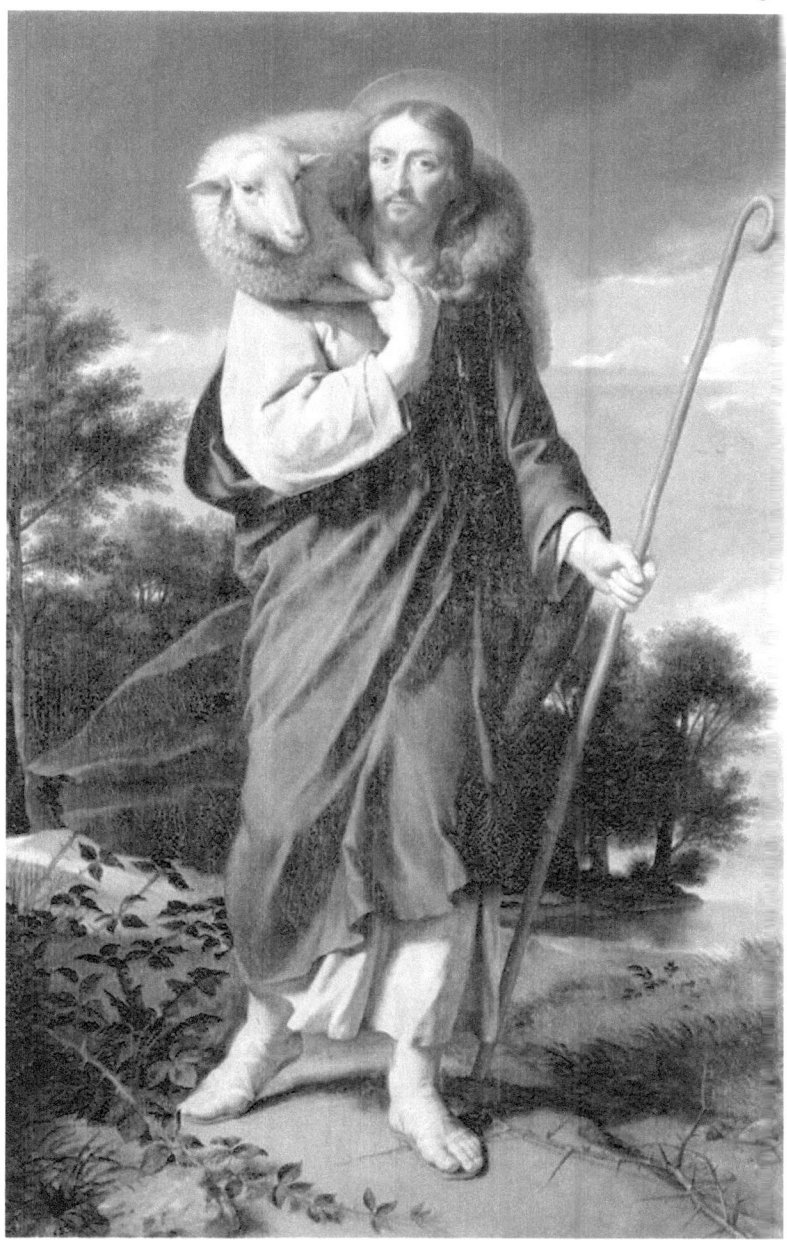

The Good Shepherd, Philippe De Champaigne[265]

---

[265] Phillipe de Champaigne, *Good Shepherd*, 1660, Oil on Canvas, 1660, L lle, Palais des Beaux-Arts de Lille,

Religion and Art

"I am the Resurrection and the Life (John 11:25-26)."

This passage tells of the resurrection of Lazarus and foreshadows the later resurrection of Jesus Himself. Andrea Vaccaro (1604-1670) captured the raising of Lazarus in his famous work *The Raising of Lazarus*, c.1630. Louisa Anne Waterford (1818-1891) portrayed a nonspecific resurrection event in *Christ Raising the Dead*. Even as our Lord made Lazarus come alive, artists can make this story come alive in the lives of people.

The resurrection of Jesus Christ is more popular. Because it is difficult to communicate in word or image, artists have approached this amazing event from a variety of angles. Mathias Grunewald (1475-1528) approached this miracle directly, painting the *Resurrection of Christ*, part of the Isenheim Altarpiece (1515). William Holman Hunt (1827-1910) emphasized the role of women in his *Christ and the two Marys*. Caravaggio (Michelangelo Merisi or Amerighi, 1571-1610) painted *Supper at Emmaus* (1606), communicating the reality of the resurrection and the humanity of the risen Lord.

"I am the Way, the Truth, and the Life (John 14:6)."

Jesus promised that not only would He rise from the dead, He would also raise up all those who believed in Him. Stanley Spencer (1891-1959) communicated this event in his *The Resurrection at Cookham* (1926), which shows saints rising from their English graves. An unknown artist-monk was more circumspect in showing how Jesus saved sinners in painting *The Descent into Hell* at the Kirillo-Belozersky Monastery. Another painter, Kriesh Aladar Korosfoi (1863-1920), created *Ego Sum Via*

---

https://upload.wikimedia.org/wikipedia/commons/1/1f/Champaigne_shepherd.jpg.

Veritas Et Vita (I Am the Way, the Truth, and the Life), in which an angel points people to Jesus.

"I am the Vine (John 15:5)."

As with "I am the door," Jesus' statement "I am the vine" is not easy to grasp. Nonetheless, Lorenzo Lotto (1480-1556) tried to reveal Jesus as the vine in his famous work *'Christ-Vine and the Legend of Saint Barbara'* (1524). Caleb Lebthy Tukahiirwa of Uganda composed a poem entitled *The True Vine* (John 15:1-12). Contemporary Christian singer John Michael Talbot performed a song called *I Am the Vine*. The vine metaphor for Christ has proved so powerful that a whole group of churches (The Vineyard Movement) has spawned from it; with over 2500 Vineyard Churches on six continents worldwide.[266]

These artists used their talents to communicate ideas about God to others, but they also used their talents to communicate the person of God to themselves. Each artist speaks first in the language that is most understandable to him. Only secondarily does the artist speak to the public. From Leonardo Da Vinci to the art teacher at the local elementary school, artists first grasp truth, then portray it to themselves, and finally portray it to others.

Even Christians who do not consider themselves artists and never produce work for public consumption reveal God through their art. A little boy finger-painting Jesus in Sunday School is using art to help him discover his Creator, and an elderly widow making a quilt for a church auction is using art to better understand her Lord. There are no "non-artists" – everyone creates art - whether a doodle on a piece of paper, a design in the snow, or a bedtime story - to accomplish a purpose. Simple acts like decorating the sanctuary or dressing up in a Chinese hat for the Lottie Moon Christmas Campaign use artistry and creativity to

---

[266] https://vineyard.org/. Accessed 9 Jan 2023

communicate eternal truths. Christians use the arts to glimpse God, and then to share that glimpse with others. Churches that powerfully shape their world for Christ with the arts encourage and enable both.

In summary, Jesus' description of Himself in His seven I AM statements comprise a description of God. We have seen that artists since the days of Rome have taken these statements and illustrated them in painting, poetry, sculpture, song, or any way that they could to reveal God to themselves and to others. They applied their talents to reveal the character and attributes of God. Both producers and consumers of this art discover the Lord in new and life changing ways.

Discussion Questions for lessons, book, and Bible studies

1. How can you communicate Jesus as the bread of life with the arts?
2. How can you communicate Jesus as the light of world with the arts?
3. How can you communicate Jesus as the door with the arts?
4. How can you communicate Jesus as the Good Shepherd with the arts?
5. How can you communicate Jesus as the Resurrection and the Life with the arts?
6. How can you communicate Jesus as the Way, the Truth, and the Life with the arts?
7. How can you communicate Jesus as the vine with the arts?
8. What does the Bible say about the beliefs and actions noted in this chapter?

17

HOW DO THE ARTS HELP SHAPE THE WORLD FOR CHRIST? BY MEETING HUMAN NEEDS

Leo Tolstoy wrote that "people who really participate in real art are morally improved (sic)." Thomas Jefferson opined that beautiful cities make for better citizens.[267] While there are counterarguments to these statements, there remains a sense of self-evidence about them. The Apostle Paul wrote that our minds should dwell on whatever is true, noble, right, good, lovely, and admirable (Philippians 4:8). Modern medicine suggests the same.

Journaling and storytelling have shown promise in the self-management of chronic pain symptoms, as has listening to music.[268] Listening to music also improves mood and arousal, which may augment performance on cognitive (thinking) tasks.[269] Playing music ("active music therapy") improves function in brain

---

[267] Ki Joo Choi, "The Deliberative Practices of Aesthetic Experience: Reconsidering the Moral Functionality of Art," *Journal of the Society of Christian Ethics* 29, no. 1 (2009): 194.
[268] Cindy Crawford, Courtney Lee, and John Bingham, "Sensory Art Therapies for the Self-Management of Chronic Pain Symptoms," *Pain Medicine* 15 (2014): S68-S69.
[269] Jens D. Rollnik and Eckart Altenmuller, "Music in Disorders of Consciousness," *Frontiers in Neuroscience* 8 (July 2014): 1.

injured patients.[270] Other studies demonstrate the efficacy of listening to music in improving patients with cancer, heart disease, and even those on mechanical ventilators.[271,272,273,274] Nature art decreases stress in children[275] and creative arts improve overall well-being in children with cancer.[276] The Cleveland Clinic found that art decreased stress, improved moods, and decreased pain in patients and others who visited.[277] Restated, just walking through hospital halls with beautiful nature-themed pictures makes those who see them healthier. Art was also useful for helping people navigate the hospital. The same is true of the Fort Belvoir

---

[270] Rollnik, 4.

[271] Joke Bradt et al., "Music Interventions for Improving Psychological and Physical Outcomes in Cancer Patients," *Cochrane Database of Systematic Reviews* 10, no. 8 (2011 Aug): 1, accessed March 11, 2016, http://www.ncbi.nlm.nih.gov/pubmed/21833957.

[272] Joke Bradt, Cheryl Dileo, and Noah Potvin, "Music for Stress and Anxiety Reduction in Coronary Heart Disease Patients," *Cochrane Database of Systematic Reviews* 12 (2013 Dec): 1, accessed March 11, 2016, http://www.ncbi.nlm.nih.gov/pubmed/?term=24374731.

[273] Joke Bradt and Cheryl Dileo, "Music Interventions for Mechanically Ventilated Patients," *Cochrane Database of Systematic Reviews* 12 (2014): 1, accessed March 11, 2016,
http://www.ncbi.nlm.nih.gov/pubmed/?term=25490233.

[274] Diana Vetter et al., "Effects of Art On Surgical Patients: A Systematic Review and Meta-Analysis," *Annals of Surgery* 262, no. 5 (November 2015): 704-13, accessed March 11, 2016,
http://www.ncbi.nlm.nih.gov/pubmed/?term=26583656.

[275] S.L. Eisen et al., "The Stress-Reducing Effects of Art in Pediatric Health Care: Art Preferences of Healthy Children and Hospitalized Children," *Journal of Child Health Care* 12, no. 3 (2008 Sep): 173-90, accessed March 11, 2016, http://www.ncbi.nlm.nih.gov/pubmed/?term=18678581.

[276] J.R. Madden et al., "Creative Arts Therapy Improves Quality of Life for Pediatric Brain Tumor Patients Receiving Outpatient Chemotherapy," *Journal of Pediatric Oncology Nursing* 27, no. 3 (2010 May-Jun): 133-45, accessed March 11, 2016, http://www.ncbi.nlm.nih.gov/pubmed/?term=20386062.

[277] M. Karnik, B. Printz, and J. Finkel, "A Hospital's Contemporary Art Collection: Effects on Patient Mood, Stress, Comfort, and Expectations," *HERD* 7, no. 3 (2014 Spring): 60-77, accessed March 11, 2016, http://www.ncbi.nlm.nih.gov/pubmed/?term=24782236.

Community Hospital, which I had the privilege of helping to design in 2007-2009, and the National Intrepid Center of Excellence for brain injured soldiers, which I helped lead in 2012-2014. One study found that green spaces (such as parks and gardens) in communities improved physical activity and even decreased overweight and obesity.[278]

One review article of the effect of the arts in medicine found many benefits:[279]

1. Music improves heart rate, respiratory rate, anxiety, relaxation, and decreases the amount of oxygen needed by the heart.
2. Visual arts improve people's sense of well-being and diminish stress and anxiety. They decrease depression and negative thoughts.
3. Movement arts improve physical symptoms, ambulation (walking), and joint range of motion. They augment overall quality of life and personal adjustment.
4. Expressive writing helps people manage anger, benefits interpersonal relationships, and decreases pain and fatigue.

A study of the use of music and scent in waiting rooms tested vanilla, mango, lavender, lemon, magnolia, and orange. It found that both music and scent reduced anxiety in patients.[280] Environments that were more homelike, less institutional, and allowed for some personalization improved behavior, well-being, social abilities, and care outcomes in patients with mental disease

---

[278] Wei-Lun Tsai et al., "Urban Vegetative Cover Fragmentation in the U.S.," *American Journal of Preventive Medicine* 50, no. 4 (April 2016): 509-17.
[279] Heather L. Stuckey and Jeremy Nobel, "The Connection between Art, Healing, and Public Health: A Review of Current Literature," *Framing Health Matters* 100, no. 2 (February 2010): 254-63.
[280] HERD. 2014 Spring;7(3):38-59. The influence of ambient scent and music on patients' anxiety in a waiting room of a plastic surgeon. Fenko A1, Loock C.

such as dementia.[281] Natural sunlight can decrease pain, stress and anxiety.[282] Several studies found that natural art reduced anxiety, pain, and medication requirements in patients, but one study found that abstract art actually worsened pain and anxiety.[283] This may be because patients did not understand the art. Windows and daylight helped improve nurses' mood, alertness, vigilance, and cognitive function in a laboratory setting. Windows and daylight also improved nurses' blood pressure and oxygen saturation (the amount of oxygen dissolved in the blood).[284] While some of this data is preliminary and needs confirmation with further studies, most of it is scientifically solid.

What do all these medical findings have to do with local churches? First, parishioners at churches often have the same kinds of medical and personal issues as patients in a clinic or hospital. Therefore, the same kind of factors can help them feel better. A man with brain damage will improve his cognitive (thought) function from listening to music in church just as he will by listening to music in a hospital. A woman with paralyzing anxiety will relax when looking at a magnificent nature scene in a church just like she will in a medical clinic. A senior citizen with crippling arthritis will feel less joint pain while in a church-sponsored dance class just as she will in a hospital-sponsored dance class.

---

[281] HERD. 2014 Fall;8(1):127-57. doi: 10.1177/193758671400800111. Impact of the design of the built environment on people with dementia: an evidence-based review. Marquardt G, Bueter K, Motzek T.
[282] HERD. 2014 Summer;7(4):108-19., Effects of environmental design on patient outcome: a systematic review. Laursen J1, Danielsen A, Rosenberg J.
[283] Ann Surg. 2015 Nov;262(5):704-13. doi: 10.1097/SLA.0000000000001480. Effects of Art on Surgical Patients: A Systematic Review and Meta-analysis. Vetter D1, Barth J, Uyulmaz S, Uyulmaz S, Vonlanthen R, Belli G, Montorsi M, Bismuth H, Witt CM, Clavien PA.
[284] HERD. 2014 Summer;7(4):35-61. The impact of windows and daylight on acute-care nurses' physiological, psychological, and behavioral health. Zadeh RS1, Shepley MM, Williams G, Chung SS.

Second, these interventions were often environmental music and art rather than formal therapy. Just as discouraged people sitting in a clinic waiting room feel better when they see lovely paintings, discouraged people sitting in a church foyer will feel better when they see lovely paintings. The concept of biophilia suggests that people who experience a natural environment, whether a forest, lake, beach, or something else, gain better health, even if they only see a photograph. Whether people have diagnosed medical conditions or not, wise use of the arts will improve their lives.

Gardens and water features are especially good for improving the health of those who experience them. The Veterans' Administration hospital in Washington DC has gardens for veterans to walk through but also opportunities to garden. Experience has shown that planting flowers and vegetables, trimming bushes, digging, and other gardening tasks improve veterans' physical and mental well-being. Many churches have the resources to do similar things.

Discussion Questions for lessons, book, and Bible studies

1. Give an example of how the arts have met your needs.
2. Give an example of how you have seen the arts help with others' needs.
3. How could your church or other organization meet human needs using the arts?
4. How can you help meet the needs of others using your skills in art, even if those skills are limited to unconventional arts such as cooking?
5. What does the Bible say about the beliefs and actions noted in this chapter?

18

Conclusion

To many Christians and non-Christians alike, the world seems to grow ever colder. The Judeo-Christian garment of cultural consensus which covered the West and enabled it to reach great heights of technology and power in the past four centuries, is threadbare. Unsure where to go, what to do, or even what to believe, people languish.

Every sentient creature, person, and organization shapes its environment to suit its felt needs. Ranging from food and shelter to relationships to meaning, we consciously and unconsciously change ourselves and our surroundings to accomplish our goals. Adherents of religions and philosophies do the same. Muslims, Hindus, Buddhists, Secular Humanists, and others shape their world, including through art, to promote their belief systems.

The Church exists to shape the world for Jesus Christ. Through evangelism, discipleship, and acting as a safeguard for culture, the Church is intended to demonstrate salvation to all and to be a blessing to the world. Art is a powerful means to shape one's environment. The Church has shaped the world for Christ using art from the Roman Empire through the Middle Ages, Renaissance, and Modern Era.

The arts shape the world by teaching ethics and morality. The arts also work through building communities. Art powerfully reveals the person of God. Finally, art can directly and indirectly

Conclusion

meet human needs. God Himself created man to benefit from noble arts performed with excellence.

Churches can use the arts to accomplish all these goals in their congregations and communities. They can incorporate windows, gardens, and photographs to maximize their members' exposure to the natural world. They can use art, whether paintings, statuary, or the like to elicit positive emotions. They can provide music and dance ministries to help heal their congregants with a variety of medical and personal problems. None of these interventions are panaceas, but each improves many aspects of peoples' lives.

Though times may seem dark to many, and the Church may seem to be in retreat, God remains in control. His Church cannot fail because He will not allow it. Christians remain salt and light in a rotting world because that is what He made us for. This book has attempted first to educate its readers about the arts, an important means to shape the world for Christ. Second, I have tried to educate readers about religions and philosophies, and how they follow their own agendas in shaping the world against the Risen One. Finally, I have endeavored to encourage readers, individually and as churches, to use the arts to shape the world for Jesus Christ.

APPENDIX 1
SUMMARIES OF RELIGIONS AND PHILOSOPHIES

Table 1 - Summary of Islamic Beliefs[285]

Topic	Belief
Creation	Allah created the universe, including man, out of nothing
Scripture and Authority	Allah recited the *Quran* in Arabic as his perfect revelation to and ultimate authority over man. Hadiths, which are sayings and actions of Mohammad, are of lesser authority. No other book, including the Bible, is reliable.
God	Monotheist, Allah is an all-powerful, all-knowing, personal god
Mankind	Possesses dignity, but not made in the image of Allah
Sin	Man has no sinful nature but does have a lower (animal) nature. Acting under the animal nature constitutes rebellion against Allah. Man uses his free will to obey Allah.
Salvation	People atone for their sin with sincere confessions and good works, including the pillars of Islam. Allah judges men at death and even the

---

[285] House, Chart 44.

	most pious may not make it to paradise. Only a martyr in jihad (holy war) is assured of salvation.
Afterlife	On the final day of judgment, people will be resurrected to Paradise or Hell. Paradise is a well-watered garden populated with beautiful virgins for the pleasure of Muslim men. Hell is a place of eternal torment for all non-Muslims.
Theophanies	Allah is distant, not intimate. Allah is a dispassionate judge. Allah hates those who disobey him.
Jihad	There are two meanings: striving against sin in one's own life, and fighting physically against kafir, "infidels."
Five Pillars	*Shahadah* (confession), *salat* (prayers), *sawm* (fasting), *zakat* (almsgiving), and *hajj* (pilgrimage to Mecca)

Religion and Art

Table 2 – Outline of Islamic History

570	Birth of Mohammad
610	Initial Revelations of the *Quran*
622	In the *Hijra*, Mohammad and his followers flee Mecca and move to Medina
624	Muslim victory over Medinan forces at Badr
630	Mecca falls
632	Mohammad dies
632-661	Rashidun Caliphate
636	Battle of Yarmuk and the Byzantine loss of Syria and the Holy Land
636	Battle of Qadisiya and the Fall of the Sassanid Persian Empire
641	Battle of Alexandria and the Muslim conquest of Egypt
661-750	Umayyad Caliphate
711	Battle of Guadalete and the Fall of Christian Spain
732	Defeat of the Moorish (Muslim) invasion of France in the Battle of Tours
750-1258	Abbasid Caliphate
8th Century	Establishment of classic Islamic jurisprudence
763-809	Golden age of Muslim civilization under Harun al Rashid
846	Writing of the Sahih al Bukhari, the most accepted compilation of Mohammad's statements
909-1171	Fatimid Caliphate
1095-1291	The Crusades to the Holy Land
1299-1922	Ottoman Empire
1453	Fall of Constantinople and the Byzantine Empire
1492	Fall of Muslim Spain
1529	Defeat of the Turks at the Siege of Vienna
12th to 18th Centuries	Muslim armies invade, conquer, and rule the Indian subcontinent
20th century	World Wars I and II, end of European colonialism and rise of Muslim Sharia states

Appendix 1

Table 3 - Summary of Hindu Beliefs[286]

Topic	Belief
Creation	The universe is an emanation of the eternal, impersonal life force known as Brahman. It has male and female aspects.
Scripture and Authority	*Sruti* (revealed) – Vedas (*Rig, Atharva, Sama, Yajur*), Upanishads *Smrti* (remembered) – *Puranas, sutras*, epics (*Ramayana, Mahabrata*), *Bhagavad-Gita*.
God	Polytheist, monotheist, monist, or atheist. Atman/Brahman is the universal spirit
Mankind	Man has an imperishable soul and perishable body. The soul transmigrates from body to body through the cycle of births and deaths (reincarnation, samsara). He lives each life in a caste (social group).
Sin	Man errs by *avidya* (ignorance) and *maya* (illusions of reality). There is no sinful nature.
Salvation	Man lives countless lives trying to break free (*moksha*) from the cycle of existence (*samsara*) by good works and knowledge of reality.
Afterlife	If the person has not achieved moksha, his or her soul is reborn in another body to continue the cycle. If he or she has, the soul is submerged into the eternal spirit (*Atman-Brahman*)
Forehead mark	Females wear a dot in the middle of their forehead to signal that they are devout Hindus, black for unmarried women and red for married ones
Debts in life	Debt to god, debt to saints and gurus, and debt to ancestors. These are all repaid with good works and faithful religious service
Five Castes	Brahmin (priest, scholar), Kshatriya (royal, military), Vaishya (businessperson, farmer), Sudra (manual laborer and servant), Dalit

[286] House, Chart 58.

Religion and Art

	(untouchable, outside of caste system). Every non-Hindu is therefore an untouchable.
Ten Observances	*Indriya nigraha* – subduing senses and sexual urges *Asteya* – refraining from theft and selfishness. *Akrodha* – controlling anger *Kshama* – forgiving others *Saucham* – purity and truthfulness *Dama* – self-restraint and contentment *Dhruti* - steadfastness *Satya* – truth and social justice *Dhee* – right understanding of Hindu scripture *Vidya* – knowledge of the divine
Four stages of Hindu life	*Brahmacharya Ashrama* – student, age 0-25 *Grhastha Ashrama* – householder, age 25-50 *Vanaprastha Ashrama* – withdrawing from society, age 50-75 Sannyasa Ashrama – meditation and preparation to die, age 75+
Four ends of Hindu life	*Dharma* (duty and righteousness), *artha* (wealth), *kama* (pleasure), *moksha*
Yoga	Exercising strict control over mind and body.

Appendix 1

Table 4 – Outline of Hindu History

2000-1500 BC	Migration/war of the Aryans from Central Asia into the Indian subcontinent
1000-1500 BC	Writing the *Vedas*
800-300 BC	Writing of the *Upanishads*
350 BC – AD 650	Malava Empire
326 BC	Alexander the Great defeated Indian forces in the Battle of the Hydaspes, conquering western India
261 BC	Maurya Empire (Buddhist) under Ashoka defeats the state of Kalinga (Hindu)
200-100 BC	Writing of the *Bhagavad Gita*
AD 240 – 550	Gupta Empire
275-897	Palava Empire
1336-1646	Vijayanagara Empire
1674-1818	Maratha Empire
1757	British defeat French, Hindu and Muslim coalition at the Battle of Plassey
1914-1918	Indian involvement in World War I
1941-1945	Indian involvement in World War 2
1947	Independence of India, Pakistan, and Bangladesh from British colonial rule
21st century	India is a rising power, and Hindu nationalism (*Hindutva*) also on the rise

Religion and Art

Table 5 - Summary of Buddhist Beliefs[287]

Topic	Belief
Creation	No material creation, as reality consists of relations rather than substances
Scripture and Authority	*Tipitaka* (Pali Canon) – *Vinaya* (monastic regulations), Sutta (general principles), and *Abhidhamma* (basic teachings) Theraveda Buddhism recognizes only the *Tipitaka*. Mahayana Buddhism adds many sutras (heart, diamond, lotus, etc.). *Vajrayana* (Tibetan) includes kangjur and tanjur.
God	God is a force, not a personal being, in most of Buddhism. In Pure Land (Chinese) Buddhism, *Amitaba* Buddha may be worshipped as god. Some ascribe god-like qualities to the Buddha (Gautama).
Mankind	There may or may not be a soul. A combination of "properties" transmigrates from body to body in reincarnation.
Sin	Sin is ignorance of the true nature of reality. Good and evil are ultimately the same.
Salvation	Eightfold path – right views (Buddhist), right resolve (eliminating improper thoughts), right speech (clear and truthful), right conduct, right livelihood (certain jobs are excluded), right effort (detached from the world), right awareness, right concentration
Afterlife	Through good works and good beliefs, Buddhists attain enlightenment, which includes liberation from illusion, detachment from desire, and a cessation of suffering. Nirvana is the endless bliss of nothingness. Those who do not attain enlightenment are reborn into another earthly life (human or animal) or go to hell. However, even those in hell can again try to climb the ladder into Nirvana

---

[287] House, Chart 67.

Buddha	"Buddha" is a title meaning teacher. There are thousands of Buddhas, defined as people who have attained enlightenment, in existence, though not necessarily on earth.
Four boundless states	Realizing that oneself is an illusion and that each individual is simply part of existence leads to love, compassion, joy, and even-temperedness
Buddhist shrines	Places to house images or representations of a Buddha
Three marks of conditioned existence	*Anatman* – no self *Anitya* – all things and experiences are impermanent. *Duhkya* – people who do not grasp anatman and anitya face endless suffering

Table 6 – Outline of Buddhist History

563 BC	Birth of Siddhartha Gautama, who later became the Buddha
483 BC	Death of Siddhartha Gautama
Around 400 BC	First Buddhist Council
Around 300 BC	Second Buddhist Council, and the split between the Theraveda and Mahayana Buddhism
322-184 BC	Maurya Empire (Buddhist) reigns in India
250 BC	Third Buddhist Council
2nd Century BC to 6th Century AD	Spread of Buddhism to China, Sri Lanka, Southeast Asia, Greece, Central Asia, and Japan
25 BC	Fourth Buddhist Council
AD 30-375	Kushan empire and Buddhism in northwestern India
20th Century	World wars, end of Western colonialism and independence of many Buddhist majority states
21st Century	Rise of China and Buddhist states in multipolar world

Appendix 1

Table 7 - Summary of Secular Humanist Beliefs[288]

Topic	Belief
Creation	Either the material universe is eternal or not. If not, it came into existence via a natural (non-divine) process. It is likely that multiple universes exist.
Scripture and Authority	Rejects all holy books and sacred texts except as they conform to the secular humanist world view. Human reason is the highest authority.
God	Either He does not exist (atheism) or He is uninvolved with the universe (deism).
Mankind	Humans result from evolutionary processes and lack intentionality. Humans have dignity, at least most of them. Some believe that man has an immaterial portion (a soul or spirit), some do not.
Sin	There is no transcendent ground for morality, so human consensus is the only standard of right and wrong. Man is born basically good.
Salvation	The only salvation needed and possible is human progress in science and justice
Afterlife	None
Anti-supernaturalism	There is nothing outside material substance (matter)
Skepticism	Nothing in any holy book is taken on faith. Everything in them is considered wrong
Humanist universalism	Social justice is the most important thing in the world

---

[288] House, Chart 54.

Appendix 2
Great Works of Christian Art[289]

Title	Artist	Time
Catacomb paintings	Unknown	c. 300
Book of Kells	Unknown	c. 550
Gregorian Chant (choral)	Unknown	c. 580
Ordo Virtutem (choral)	Hildegard of Bingen	
Chartres Cathedral	Unknown	1134
The Windows of Saint Chapelle		
The Divine Comedy (poem)	Dante	1320
The Scrovegni Chapel Frescoes	Giotto	1305
The Holy Trinity icon (painting)	Andrei Rublev	1410
The Adoration of the Lamb (painting)	Jan van Eck	1432
The Four Horsemen of the Apocalypse (woodcut)	Albrecht Durer	1498
The Garden of Earthly Delights (painting)	Hieronymus Bosch	c. 1500
The Ceiling of the Sistine Chapel (painting)	Michelangelo	1508-12
A Mighty Fortress is our God (hymn)	Martin Luther	1529
The Procession to Calvary (painting)	Pieter Brueghel	1564

---

[289] 75 Masterpieces every Christian should know

Appendix 2

The Burial of the Count of Orgaz (painting)	El Greco	1586
The Incredulity of Saint Thomas	Caravaggio	1601-2
The Holy Sonnets (poems)	John Donne	1633
The Temple (poems)	George Herbert	1633
Agnus Dei (painting)	Francisco de Zurbaran	1635-1640

Religion and Art

Great Works of Christian Art (2)

Title	Artist	Time
St. Teresa in Ecstasy (sculpture)	Bernini	1652
The Return of the Prodigal Son (painting)	Rembrandt	1669
The Pilgrim's Progress (novel)	John Bunyan	1678
When I Survey the Wondrous Cross (hymn)	Isaac Watts	1707
St. Matthew's Passion (oratorio)	J.S. Bach	1727
Messiah (oratorio)	Georg Friderich Handel	1741
Amazing Grace (hymn)	John Newton	1779
Songs of Innocence and Experience (poems)	William Blake	1789-1794
The Creation (oratorio)	Franz Joseph Haydn	1798
Pride and Prejudice (novel)	Jane Austin	1813
The Wanderer Above the Sea of Fog (painting)	Caspar David Friedrich	1818
Symphony 5, The Reformation	Felix Mendelssohn	1830
The Voyage of Life (painting)	Thomas Cole	1842
The Light of the World (painting)	William Holman Hunt	1854
The Heart of the Andes (painting)	Frederic Edwin Church	1859
Fairy Tales (stories)	George MacDonald	1871
The Brothers Karamazov (novel)	Fyodor Dostoyevsky	1879
La Sagrada Familia Cathedral	Antoni Gaudi	1882
Starry Night (painting)	Vincent Van Gogh	1889

Appendix 2

Great Works of Christian Art (3)

Title	Artist	Time
The Life of our Lord Jesus Christ (painting)	James Tissot	1896
The Annunciation (painting)	Henry Ossawa Tanner	1898
The Complete Poems	Emily Dickinson	1890
The Innocence of Father Brown (short stories)	G.K. Chesterton	1911
The Life of Christ (painting)	Emil Nolde	1912
Poems	Gerard Manly Hopkins	1918
The Resurrection at Cookham (painting)	Stanley Spencer	1926
Death Comes for the Archbishop (novel)	Willa Catther	1927
The Passion of Joan of Arc (film)	Theodore Dreyer	1928
Head of Christ (painting)	Georges Rouault	1937
The Power and the Glory (novel)	Graham Greene	1940
Quartet for the End of Time	Olivier Messiaen	1941
Four Quartets (poems)	T.S. Eliot	1943
The Man Born to be King (drama)	Dorothy L. Sayers	1943
Rome, Open City (film)	Roberto Rossellini	1945
It's a Wonderful Life (film)	Frank Capra	1946
I Will Move on Up a Little Higher (music)	Mahalia Jackson	1947

Religion and Art

Great Works of Christian Art (4)

Title	Artist	Time
The Chronicles of Narnia (novel)	C.S. Lewis	1950-1956
The Lord of the Rings (novel)	JRR Tolkien	1954-1955
A Love Supreme (music)	John Coltrane	1964
Au Hasard du Balthasar (film)	Robert Bresson	1966
Andrei Rublev (film)	Andrei Tarkovsky	1966
Cancer Ward (novel)	Aleksandr Solzhenitsyn	1967
At Folsom Prison (music)	Johnny Cash	1968
The Complete Stories	Flannery O'Connor	1971
Only Visiting this Planet (music)	Larry Norman	1972
The Symphony of Sorrowful Songs	Henryk Gorecki	1976
Dancing in the Dragon's Jaws (music)	Bruce Cockburn	1979
The Second Coming (novel)	Walker Percy	1980
The Last Supper (print)	Sadao Watanabe	1981
Godric (novel)	Frederick Buechner	1981
Infidels (music)	Bob Dylan	1983
The Joshua Tree (music)	U2	1987
Paradise Garden	Howard Finster	1990
The Four Holy Gospels (painting)	Makoto Fujimura	2011
The Tree of Life (film)	Terrence Malik	2011

Appendix 3
Using This Book in Sermons, Classrooms, and Other Teaching Occasions.

Pastors, professors, teachers, parents, homeschoolers, and others can use any part of this book, from world religions to philosophy to history to the arts, in their sermons, discussions, and other teaching occasions. There are several characteristics which make this book amenable to such uses:

1. Images herein can illustrate single points in a sermon. Art is easier to find with the electronic version of this book. Owners of the print book can simply search for the name of the piece on the internet.
2. Images herein can be the topic of entire sermons, multiple points rather than just one. For example, Rembrandt's Prodigal Son is a famous painting of a famous parable, in which all three characters exemplify a different problem, and the progression of growth in a human life.
3. The citations are exhaustive for any topic covered in this book. The bibliography thus provides a pathway to further research.
4. The discussion questions guide teachers and group facilitators as they reveal a wide variety of truths to their students.
5. The tables in the appendices reveal key points on each topic worthy of further investigation.

Religion and Art

6. The widespread use of transliterations of texts in other languages (i.e., Sanskrit, Pali) is intended to provide the pastor/teacher with a reliable way to clearly understand and further investigate the underlying concepts.
7. Cultural issues in major religions, such as wedding rituals, writing, and music, fit handily into a curriculum on world cultures or missions.
8. The list of great works of Christian art is extensive and makes a good multipart study.
9. Some concepts and images contained herein are most appropriate for adults, youth, and perhaps older children. Teacher and parent discretion is recommended.

Bibliography

al-Misri, Ahmad ibn Naqib. *Reliance of the Traveller: the Classic Manual of Islamic Sacred Law 'umdat Al-Salik*. Rev. ed. Edited by Nuh Ha Mim Keller. Beltsville, MD: Amana Corporation, 1999.

Arnett, Lloyd. "The Sacred Precinct: Reclaiming the Place of the Christian Humanist Tradition of Theatre Art in the 21st Century Intellectual Community." *Baylor Journal of Theatre and performance* 1, no. 1 (Fall 2004): 69-76. Accessed March 11, 2016. http://eds.b.ebscohost.com.ezproxy.sbts.edu/ehost/pdfviewer/pdfviewer?vid=3&sid=c49ac157-226c-4d35-88c5-cd22f5319998%40sessionmgr113&hid=121.

Bailey, Mark S., and H. Janaka de Silva. "Sri Lankan Sanni Masks: An Ancient Classification of Disease." *British Medical Journal* 333.7582 (2006): 1327-28.

Begbie, Jeremy. *Music, Modernity, and God: Essays in Listening*. Oxford: Oxford University Press, 2013.

Benedict, Saint. *The Rule of Saint Benedict*. Vintage Spiritual Classics. NY: Random House, 1981.

Berding, Kenneth. "The Crisis of Biblical Illiteracy," *Biola Magazine*, June 2014, 1, accessed June 19, 2017, http://magazine.biola.edu/article/14-spring/the-crisis-of-biblical-illiteracy/.

Religion and Art

Berger, Helen A., ed. *Witchcraft and Magic: Contemporary North America*. Philadelphia: University of Pennsylvania Press, 2005.

Bodhi, Bhikkhu. *The Numerical Discourses of the Buddha: A Translation of the Anguttara Nikaya*. Boston: Wisdom Publications, 2012.

Blue Book of Pianos. "US Piano Sales History from 1900 to Present." www.bluebookofpianos.com, 2012. http://www.bluebookofpianos.com/uspiano.htm.

Bokhari, Raana, Mohammed Sidiq Seddon, Charles Phillips, and Riad Nourallah. *The Illustrated Encyclopedia of Islam : A Comprehensive Guide to the History, Philosophy and Practice of Islam around the World, with More than 500 Beautiful Illustrations*. London: Lorenz Books, 2009.

Borstein, Michelle. "Sen. Raphael Warnock's Deleted Easter Tweet Reflects Religious and Political Chasms about Christianity." *Washington Post*, April 5, 2021. https://www.washingtonpost.com/religion/2021/04/05/raphael-warnock-deletes-tweet-easter-resurrection-jeremiah-wright/.

Bradt, Joke, Cheryl Dileo, Densie Grocke, and Lucanne Magill. "Music Interventions for Improving Psychological and Physical Outcomes in Cancer Patients." *Cochrane Database of Systematic Reviews* 10, no. 8 (2011 Aug): 1. Accessed March 11, 2016. http://www.ncbi.nlm.nih.gov/pubmed/21833957.

Bradt, Joke, Cheryl Dileo, and Noah Potvin. "Music for Stress and Anxiety Reduction in Coronary Heart Disease Patients." *Cochrane Database of Systematic Reviews* 12 (2013 Dec): 1. Accessed March 11, 2016. http://www.ncbi.nlm.nih.gov/pubmed/?term=24374731.

Bradt, Joke, and Cheryl Dileo. "Music Interventions for Mechanically Ventilated Patients." *Cochrane Database of Systematic Reviews* 12 (2014): 1. Accessed March 11,

2016. http://www.ncbi.nlm.nih.gov/pubmed/?term=25490233.

Brown, John Russell, ed. *The Oxford Illustrated History of Theatre*. New York: Oxford University Press, 2001.

Brown, Michelle P. *The Lion Companion to Christian Art*. Oxford: Lion Hudson, 2008.

Byfield, Ted, and Paul Stanway, eds. *The Christians: Their First Two Thousand Years*. Vol. 6, *The Quest for the City A.D. 740 to 1100*. Edmonton: Christian History Project, Inc., 2004.

Chaves, Mark. "What Do Congregations Do? the Significance of Christian Congregations to American Civic Life." *Word and World* 27, no. 3 (sum 2007): 295-304. Accessed March 11, 2016. http://eds.b.ebscohost.com.ezproxy.sbts.edu/ehost/pdfviewer/pdfviewer?sid=c49ac157-226c-4d35-88c5-cd22f5319998%40sessionmgr113&vid=10&hid=121.

Choi, Ki Joo. "The Deliberative Practices of Aesthetic Experience: Reconsidering the Moral Functionality of Art." *Journal of the Society of Christian Ethics* 29, no. 1 (2009): 193-218.

Corichi, Manolo. "Eight-In-Ten Indians Limit Meat in Their Diets, and Four-In-Ten Consider Themselves Vegetarian." Pew Research Center, July 8, 2021. https://www.pewresearch.org/short-reads/2021/07/08/eight-in-ten-indians-limit-meat-in-their-diets-and-four-in-ten-consider-themselves-vegetarian/.

Crawford, Cindy, Courtney Lee, and John Bingham. "Sensory Art Therapies for the Self-Management of Chronic Pain Symptoms." *Pain Medicine* 15 (2014): S66-S75.

Dillenberger, John, ed. *Martin Luther: Selections from His Writings*. New York: Doubleday, 1962.

https://www.dramashare.org/.

Dyrness, William A. *Visual Faith: Art, Theology, and Worship in Dialogue*. Grand Rapids, MI: Baker Academic, 2001.

Eknath Easwaran. *The Upanishads*. ReadHowYouWant.com, 2010.

Eck, Diana L. *Darśan: Seeing the Divine Image in India*. 3rd ed. New York: Columbia University Press, 1998.

Eisen, S.L., R.S. Ulrich, M.M. Shepley, J.W. Varni, and S. Sherman. "The Stress-Reducing Effects of Art in Pediatric Health Care: Art Preferences of Healthy Children and Hospitalized Children." *Journal of Child Health Care* 12, no. 3 (2008 Sep): 173-90. Accessed March 11, 2016. http://www.ncbi.nlm.nih.gov/pubmed/?term=18678581.

Elgood, Heather. *Hinduism and the Religious Arts*. Religion and the Arts. London: Cassell, 2000.

Embree, Ainslie, and Stephen Hay, eds. *Sources of Indian Tradition*. 2nd ed. Vol. 1, *From the Beginning to 1800 (Introduction to Oriental Civilizations)*. New York: Columbia University Press, 1988.

Eschrich, Susann, Thomas F. Munte, and Eckart O. Altenmuller. "Unforgettable Film Music: The Role of Emotion in Episodic Long-Term Memory for Music." *BMC Neuroscience* 9, no. 48 (28 May 2008): 1-7. Accessed March 11, 2016. http://bmcneurosci.biomedcentral.com/articles/10.1186/1471-2202-9-48.

Fell Mcdermott, Rachel, Leonard A Gordon, Ainslie T Embree, Frances W Pritchett, and Dennis Dalton. *Sources of Indian Traditions Modern India, Pakistan, and Bangladesh*. New York Chichester, West Sussex: Columbia University Press, 2014.

Glaspey, Terry. *75 Masterpieces Every Christian Should Know: the Fascinating Stories Behind Great Works of Art, Literature, Music, and Film*. Grand Rapids, MI: Baker Books, 2015.

Griffith, Ralph T H, Arthur Berriedale Keith, and Jon William Fergus. *The Vedas: The Saṃhitās of the Ṛig, Yajur (White *and Black), Sāma, and Atharva Vedas*. United States: Kshetra Books, 2017.

Haddad, Yvonne Yazbeck, and Jane I. Smith, eds. *The Oxford Handbook of American Islam*. Oxford Handbooks. New York: Oxford University Press, 2014.

Hamilton, Edith, and Steele Savage. *Mythology*. A Mentor Book. New York: New American Library, 1969.

Harvey, Peter. *An Introduction to Buddhism: Teachings, History and Practices*. second ed. [introduction to Religion]. Cambridge: Cambridge University Press, 2013.

Hillenbrand, Robert. *Islamic Art and Architecture*. World of Art. New York: Thames and Hudson, 1999.

Hodgson, Marshall G S. *The Venture of Islam: Conscience and History in a World Civilization*. Chicago: University of Chicago Press, 1974.

House, H Wayne. *Charts of World Religions*. Zondervan Charts. Grand Rapids: Zondervan, 2006.

Ibn al-Naqīb, Aḥmad ibn Lu'lu'. *Reliance of the Traveller: The Classic Manual of Islamic Sacred Law 'umdat Al-Salik*. Rev. ed. Translated by Noah Ha Mim Keller. Beltsville, MD: Amana Publications, 2011.

Josephus, Flavius. *Josephus: The Complete Works*. Translated by William Whiston. Nashville: Thomas Nelson Inc, 1998.

Karnik, M., B. Printz, and J. Finkel. "A Hospital's Contemporary Art Collection: Effects On Patient Mood, Stress, Comfort, and Expectations." *HERD* 7, no. 3 (2014 Spring): 60-77. Accessed March 11, 2016. http://www.ncbi.nlm.nih.gov/pubmed/?term=24782236.

Khadduri, Majid. *The Islamic Conception of Justice*. Baltimore: Johns Hopkins University Press, 2003.

Kilde, Jeanne Halgren. *Sacred Power, Sacred Space: an Introduction to Christian Architecture and Worship*. Oxford: Oxford University Press, 2008.

Lemons, J. Stanley. *First: The First Baptist Church in America.* Providence, RI: The Charitable Baptist Society, 2001.

L'Engle, Madeleine. *A Full House.* Shaw, 2000.

Levitin, Daniel J. *This is your Brain on Music, the Science of a Human Obsession.* New York: Penguin Group, 2006.

Madden, Deborah. "Medicine and Moral Reform: The Place of Practical Piety in John Wesley's Art of Physic." *The American Society of Church History* 73, no. 4 (2004): 741-58.

Madden, J.R., P. Mowry, D. Gao, P.M. Cullen, and N.K. Foreman. "Creative Arts Therapy Improves Quality of Life for Pediatric Brain Tumor Patients Receiving Outpatient Chemotherapy." *Journal of Pediatric Oncology Nursing* 27, no. 3 (2010 May-Jun): 133-45. Accessed March 11, 2016. http://www.ncbi.nlm.nih.gov/pubmed/?term=20386062.

Magliocco, Sabina. *Witching Culture: Folklore and Neo-Paganism in America.* Contemporary Ethnography. Philadelphia: University of Pennsylvania Press, 2004.

McNamara, Denis R. *How to Read Churches: A Crash Course in Ecclesiastical Architecture.* New York: Rizzoli International Publishers, 2011.

McNeill, William H. *Keeping Together in Time: Dance and Drill in Human History.* Cambridge MA: Harvard University Press, 1995.

Michell, George. *The Hindu Temple: An Introduction to Its Meaning and Forms.* Chicago: University of Chicago Press, 1988.

Mordecai, Carolyn. *Weddings, Dating, and Love Customs of Cultures Worldwide.* Phoenix AZ: Nittany Publishers, 1999.

O' Callaghan, Regan. Quoted in Michelle P. Brown, *The Lion Companion to Christian Art.* Oxford: Lion Hudson, 2008

Parrinder, Geoffrey. *Sexual Morality in the World's Religions*. Oxford, England: Oneworld Publications, 1996.

Pew Research Center. "Key Findings from the Global Religious Futures Project." Pew Research Center, December 21, 2022. https://www.pewresearch.org/religion/2022/12/21/key-findings-from-the-global-religious-futures-project/.

Pluckrose, Helen, and James Lindsay. *Cynical Theories: How Activist Scholarship Made Everything about Race, Gender, and Identity-and Why This Harms Everybody*. Durham, North Carolina: Pitchstone Publishing, 2020.

Pole, Sebastian. *Ayurvedic Medicine: The Principles of Traditional Practice*. Philadelphia: Singing Dragon, Cop, 2013.

Porter Jr., H. Boone. "God, Art, and Satan." *Anglican Theological Review* 29, no. 4 (October 1947): 242-46. Accessed March 11, 2016. http://eds.b.ebscohost.com.ezproxy.sbts.edu/ehost/pdfviewer/pdfviewer?sid=c49ac157-226c-4d35-88c5-cd22f5319998%40sessionmgr113&vid=13&hid=121.

Ramanujan, Attipat Krishnaswami, David Dean Shulman, and Velcheru Narayana Rao. *When God Is a Customer: Telugu Courtesan Songs by Ksetrayya and Others*. Delhi: Oxford University Press, 1995.

Reeves, Gene, trans. *The Lotus Sutra: A Contemporary Translation of a Buddhist Classic*. Somerville, MA: Wisdom Publications, 2008.

Rollnik, Jens D., and Eckart Altenmuller. "Music in Disorders of Consciousness." *Frontiers in Neuroscience* 8 (July 2014): 1-6.

Ruthven, Malise. *Islam in the world*. 3rd ed. Oxford: Oxford University Press, 2006.

Schaeffer, Francis A. *Art and the Bible*. Downers Grove, IL: IVP Books, 2006.

Schumann, Hans Wolfgang. *The Historical Buddha: The Times, Life, and Teachings of the Founder of Buddhism*. London: Arkana, 1989.

Serrà, Joan, Álvaro Corral, Marián Boguñá, Martín Haro, and Josep Ll. Arcos. "Measuring the Evolution of Contemporary Western Popular Music." *Scientific Reports* 2, no. 1 (July 26, 2012). https://doi.org/10.1038/srep00521.

Seyyed Hossein Nasr. *The Study Quran: A New Translation and Commentary*. New York: HarperOne, An Imprint of HarperCollins Publishers, 2017.

Staufer, Ed, Jimmie R Duncan, and William Lotz. *Fire Chaplain Training Manual*. Federal of Fire Chaplains, 2005.

Stuckey, Heather L., and Jeremy Nobel. "The Connection between Art, Healing, and Public Health: A Review of Current Literature." *Framing Health Matters* 100, no. 2 (February 2010): 254-63.

Tatum, W. Barnes. *Jesus at the Movies: A Guide to the First Hundred Years (Revised) [paperback]*. 3rd ed. Salem, OR: Polebridge Pr Westar Inst, 2004.

Turner, Steve. *Imagine: A Vision for Christians in the Arts*. Downers Grove, IL: IVP Books, 2001.

Tsai, Wei-Lun, Myron F. Floyd, Yu-Fai Leung, Melissa R. McHale, and Brian J. Reich. "Urban Vegetative Cover Fragmentation in the U.S." *American Journal of Preventive Medicine* 50, no. 4 (April 2016): 509-17.

Vetter, Diana, Jurgen Barth, Sema Uyulmaz, Rene Voniathen, Giulio Belli, Marco Montorsi, Henri Bismuth, Claudia M. Witt, and Pierre-Alain Clavien. "Effects of Art On Surgical Patients: A Systematic Review and Meta-Analysis." *Annals of Surgery* 262, no. 5 (November 2015): 704-13. Accessed March 11, 2016. http://www.ncbi.nlm.nih.gov/pubmed/?term=26583656.

Wade-Matthews, Max. *The History of Musical Instruments and Music-Making: A Complete History of Musical Forms and the Orchestra*. London: Southwater, 2010.

Wilson-Dickson, Andrew. *The Story of Christian Music: from Gregorian Chant to Black Gospel: An Authoritative Illustrated Guide to All the Major Traditions of Music for Worship*. Minneapolis, MN: Fortress, 1997.

Wolterstorff, Nicholas. *Art in Action: Toward a Christian Aesthetic*. Grand Rapids: Eerdmans, 1987.

World Population Review. "Muslim Population by Country 2023." worldpopulationreview.com, 2023. https://worldpopulationreview.com/country-rankings/muslim-population-by-country.Yates, Wilson. "Literature, the Arts, and the Teaching of Ethics: The Survey." *The Annual of the Society of Christian Ethics* (1988): 225-37.

Zaehner, R C. *Hinduism*. New York: Oxford Paperbacks, 1966.

www.ingramcontent.com/pod-product-compliance
Lightning Source LLC
Chambersburg PA
CBHW020653220526
45464CB00001B/413